WIRED *for* MINISTRY

FIRST EDITION

Ronald E. Ovitt

GILGAL PUBLISHING
12540 S. 68th Ct.
Palos Heights, IL 60463

Wired for Ministry

Printed in the United States of America

Unless otherwise noted, all Scripture quotations are taken from the Holy Bible, New Living Translation®, (NLT®), copyright © 1996, 2004, 2007, 2013, 2015 by Tyndale House Foundation. Used by permission of Tyndale House Publishers, Inc., Carol Stream, Illinois 60188. All rights reserved.

Gilgal Publishing
12540 S. 68th Ct.
Palos Heights, IL 60463 708-601-0113

www.empowerministry.org

Preface

My experience with spiritual gift inventories began many years ago. As a student in Bible college, a simple spiritual gift self-assessment brought clarity to my thinking and helped me choose curriculum and ministry service opportunities that solidified what I believed God wanted me to do. As a young man, I was intrigued by the dynamic way this instrument was able to confirm what I knew in my heart would be a lifetime of service.

During my graduate studies in psychology, I was compelled to learn the art and science of using self-assessments to produce self-discovery designed to guide people toward productive life changes. My ministry passions eventually settled squarely into two intertwining tracks: 1) helping Christians find their role in Christ's work in this world, and 2) helping people develop emotional resilience to bounce back from painful emotions.

Over the years, I developed a variety of self-assessments to help people get a sense of direction in their personal ministry. These inventories are presented collectively in this workbook, Wired for Ministry, and will guide you through a vigorous discovery process to identify the unique way God has equipped you for ministry.

I encourage you to pray and open your heart to God's leading as you go through this workbook. Find out how you're *Wired for Ministry*!

Ron Ovitt
Executive Director, Empower Ministry

Acknowledgments

No one writes a book by themselves. Authors are influenced by many people and experiences that have shaped their unique story. I am no exception. This book has come out of decades of ministry and working with volunteers. It also emerges from those I have served within the exciting community of faith, beginning with my original church family, Dunning Park Chapel. Although many have gone on to be with our Savior, it was at that precious chapel that I learned to love ministry.

I give thanks to all those who participated with me in Limaland Youth for Christ in Lima, Ohio. This was the beginning of my life of ministry. We were a community of believers and had a deep love for each other, many of whom I have kept in contact over the years.

Many thanks to the youth group at Immanuel Baptist Church in Waukegan, Illinois. They were such a precious group of young people. I learned so much working with them. So many have faithfully continued living for the Lord and are serving in various churches. Many of the principles taught in this book were used in that youth group.

I want to thank Pastor Howard Hoekstra, my Pastor at Calvary and a dear friend and co-minister. This is where I served as Executive Pastor and Pastor of Outreach for thirteen years. We were able to use many of the teachings from this book with the congregation. All my dear friends at Calvary Church, co-workers in ministry, had a tremendous influence on my life.

I thank the board members of Empower Ministry—Mary and George Van Dahm, Howard Hoekstra, and Janine Ovitt—for helping make this book become a reality. To all the donors to Empower Ministry, this book would not be produced without your financial help.

My thanks to Helen Olberg, a skilled computer software consultant. She went above and beyond and is responsible for making the surveys in this workbook available online.

Many thanks to my twin brother Rod Ovitt for his editing and encouragement in this project. A special thanks to his wife Carolyn Ovitt for the final layout and cover art. She is truly gifted and has been an invaluable help in coordinating book branding and graphics for our book publishing.

A special thanks to Donald Martindell, the head of the Practical Christian Ministry department at Moody Bible College. For five years I have been invited to share the contents of this book with every incoming student at Moody. It has helped to hone this message.

Writing comes out of my own journey with the Lord. My own journey, of course, is with all those who I have lived and worked with. I especially want to thank my wife and three sons who shaped me during my adulthood and supported me during some of life's severe struggles. What I have learned about life from my children and grandchildren has continually inspired my writing.

Finally, my praise goes to the Lord Jesus Christ. I pray that this book will bring Him honor and praise.

WIRED *for* MINISTRY

Contents

INTRODUCTION

Wired with a Purpose

Why am I here? What is the meaning of my life? How can I find significance? These questions are basic to our life experience. Knowing which ministries we were created for helps answer these questions. It is the compass that gives us direction on our journey. The Bible teaches that God created us and knows us personally. Jesus illustrated this concept when he used the metaphor of the shepherd and his sheep. He said that the shepherd "called" each sheep by name. Isaiah writes about this in the Old Testament. The prophet writes, "The Lord called me before my birth; from within the womb he called me by name" (Isaiah 49:1) and, "Bring all who claim me as their God, for I have made them for my glory. It was I who created them" (Isaiah 43:7). "Can a mother forget the baby at her breast and have no compassion on the child she has borne? Though she may forget, I will not forget you! See, I have engraved you on the palms of my hands" (Isaiah 49:15).

The Bible clearly teaches that God created you and me with a purpose. This purpose is perfectly exemplified in the life and teachings of Jesus Christ. In Matthew 22:36, the Pharisees asked Jesus which commandment was the greatest. They wanted to know the most important thing they should do. "Jesus replied, 'You must love the Lord your God with all your heart, all your soul, and all your mind. This is the first and greatest commandment. A second is equally important: 'Love your neighbor as yourself'" (Matthew 22:37-39).

Jesus not only *said* these words, but we know from reading the New Testament that Jesus *lived* these words. Even better, God has made it possible for you and me to live them, as well! This is the miracle of Christianity. God is able to take you and me, who so often separate ourselves from him and want nothing to do with his control in our lives and bring us into a wonderful relationship with him. That's what Jesus is all about. His life was set as an example for our own ministry, and his death and resurrection is the bridge that brings us to God. When we first realized our need for Christ and came to him in repentance and accepted him as our Savior, we began our relationship with God. It is with this relationship that we find meaning, significance, and purpose; we begin our ministry. Jesus called it, "being born again." This is when we accept the new life that God has for us and his invitation to join him in his work for this world.

The question is, how do we live out this ministry that Jesus talked about? How do we love God with all our heart, soul and mind and love our neighbor as ourselves? We do this by being

PERSONAL MINISTRY

MINISTRY IS TO LIVE WITH THE WARENESS OF THE PRESENCE, LOVE AND POWER OF THE RISEN CHRIST, USING OUR PERSONHOOD, GIFTS AND SKILLS TO SERVE HIM IN EVERYTHING WE DO.

1

aware of God's presence in our lives, the love he has for us, and the power that he wants to use. This moves our heart, soul, and mind into action. We then love our neighbor by serving God with everything we have and in everything we do.

AWARENESS OF THE PRESENCE, LOVE AND POWER OF THE RISEN CHRIST.

Awareness of God is the first stage in developing our personal ministry. We are living for God. Not just *a* god, but the *living* God. What a difference! We're not living out some religious experience—we've entered into a relationship with the risen Christ. So often we treat Jesus like another historic figure. We meet on Sundays to remember his death, we sing his praises for what he has done and then go about our week as if his present risen-ness has no bearing on our lives. For a vibrant ministry, we must have a vital relationship with the risen Christ, one that influences every aspect of our lives. This realization results in a transformation that empowers our psyche and, in turn, the results of our ministry. He is alive. And the same power that rose Jesus from the dead is available for our ministry. Living every hour of every day in the conscious awareness of the love of Jesus gives hope and peace. The risen Jesus motivates, inspires, gives courage, and leads us in the way that we should go.

USING OUR PERSONHOOD, GIFTS AND SKILLS.

Using our personal gifts and skills for God is a deliberate choice to be cognizant of all that we are, live for all that he is, and be mindful of all that needs to be done. We ask ourselves, "What is my part? What is my role in this drama of life?" We find the answer when we come to the realization that God has given us a unique combination of personality, interests, spiritual gifts, and aptitudes that we can use for him. There are many factors that make us who we are. Each of these variables combines to produce the outcome of our unique selves.

PERSONAL TRAITS	ENVIRONMENT	BELIEF SYSTEM
Genes, personality, temperament, chemistry, intelligence, birth order, physical abilities and limitations, aptitudes, and the spiritual gifts that God gives you.	Parenting, siblings, relatives, social status, neighborhood, school, clubs, church, civic groups, sports, meaningful or tragic events in your life.	Your attitudes, core beliefs, motivations, yearnings, ambitions, presuppositions, perceptions, and predictions.

Table 1. Variables that combine to produce the outcome of our unique selves.

There are many more elements and variations of these components that make up who we are. When we consider the variables and their individual intensities, the result is an endless list of unique combinations. These combinations result in our *giftedness*.

My work and ministry are centered around our similarity and uniqueness as human beings. Perhaps it's because I'm an identical twin. I have been compared to my brother, Rod, all my life. This preoccupation with being a twin made me keenly aware of similarities and differences in individuals. As close and identical as I am with my twin, and as similar as our backgrounds are, we're still very different. We're uniquely gifted in specific ways. I find great comfort in the fact that God has never once confused me with my twin brother. I don't live out my brother's life ministry, and he doesn't live out mine. God is personal to both of us. He created us as alike as any two people can be, yet, I fulfill my everyday ministry through my own giftedness, differently than my brother.

As part of our call and ministry in life, God expects us to make the world a better place through our personhood, the spiritual gifts he has given us, and the skills we develop. Paul wrote about this in his letter to the Christians at Ephesus. "For we are God's masterpiece. He has created us anew in Christ Jesus, so we can do the good things he planned for us long ago" (Ephesians 2:10).

We are God's masterpiece or, as some translations put it, workmanship. When a pottery artisan sets out to make an object, a simple lump of clay is transformed into the object the artisan had envisioned. Our great and loving God thought about you and me individually and then intentionally created us for specific good works. We were not mass-produced; we're God's workmanship. We are the unique, one-of-a-kind ambassador that God created us to be in this world. As we respond to the life we've been given with our unique selves, as we become conscious of our ministry preferences and more proficient with the skills, abilities, and resources that God has given us, we live out the unique ministries set before us in our lives for God.

Activating Your Passions, Experience, and Abilities

S o, you want to be involved in ministry, but you're not sure what to do or where to serve. You're not alone. Sometimes people volunteer for ministries or charitable work in response to a program campaign rather than a specific calling to use their unique gifts. Often, ministry program coordinators and organizations struggle to find people who are best suited to participate in the areas of service they desperately need. It's a challenge to connect uniquely gifted people with the opportunities they have a passion for and in which they are most suited to serve.

Wired for Ministry helps both parties. You're wondering where to serve and ministries are looking for passionate, qualified volunteers. This workbook includes a suite of self-assessments organized around two dimensions—*motivation* and *background*.

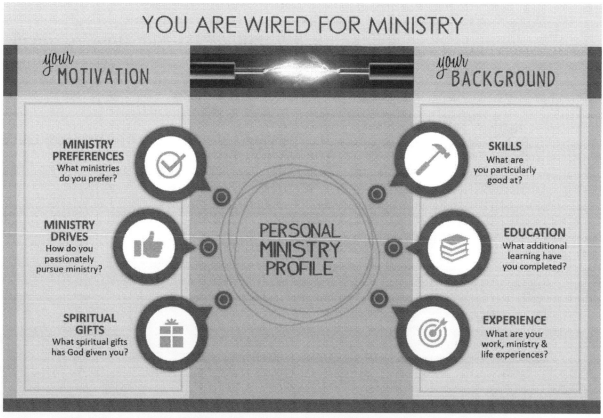

Table 2. Personal Ministry Profile used to match volunteer opportunities that will be meaningful to you and beneficial to a ministry or organization that needs your services.

When it comes to employment, you know what you're good at and can describe how you're qualified for a job that's been posted. You also know what kinds of jobs you wouldn't be good at or interested in pursuing. But when it comes to volunteering, you may not think your passions or experience are important, and you may not know how you've been uniquely gifted and equipped for ministry. Whether you volunteer with a church, non-profit agency, or local charity, our goal is to create the best possible experience for you and the organization you volunteer for.

You wouldn't think of applying for a job without gathering information for the application and updating your resume. You need to identify your attributes and aptitudes for personal ministry in the same way you would prepare for employment, and we developed a systematic process to help you do just that. It's called your *Personal Ministry Profile,* and it will guide you through a methodical analysis of your personal passions, experience, and abilities.

YOUR UNIQUE SELF

This workbook includes self-assessment inventories that will help you reflect on how you've been uniquely created by God for ministry. He has given you skills, abilities, and passions that can be used to advance causes and help in many different ministries. At the end of the process, you'll have a comprehensive overview of your unique combination of personality, interests, spiritual gifts, and aptitudes that you can use to serve God. With this information, you'll be able to meet with ministry leaders at your church or the director of volunteer services at your favorite charity. Together, you'll identify specific volunteer opportunities that will allow the organization to take full advantage of your gifts and abilities and allow you to serve the Lord in a way that energizes you and brings you deep joy.

The information you gather using *Wired for Ministry* tools will set you apart as a committed, prepared volunteer and help you and the organization find the perfect fit for your unique self. The results will be captured in your Personal Ministry Profile and will help you to match your gifts, passions, and aptitudes to specific areas of service that are commonly needed in ministry and charitable organizations.

THE PERSONAL MINISTRY PLANNING PROCESS

Think of the Personal Ministry Profile as a resume. You want to serve where you're energized and can make an impact. The person reading it will be able to see the passion, experience, and abilities you bring to the task at hand, and it will provide them with your contact information and references. When completed, your profile will contain the summary results from each of the six assessment areas and give you a valuable at-a-glance overview to use in determining the volunteer opportunities you'd like to pursue.

When trying to determine how to use the personal skills and abilities God gave you, there are two things you should do that will help you make a well-informed decision. First, you need to examine your *background*—the skills, education, and experience you have that can be used in ministry. Then, you need to discover your *motivation*—how spiritual gifts, ministry drives, and ministry preferences uniquely equip you for ministry. These are Steps One and Two of the *Personal Ministry Planning* process.

In Step One, you'll use three different inventories to examine the skills, education, and experience you have that can be used in ministry. In Step Two, you'll complete three additional inventories to discover how your spiritual gifts, ministry drives, and ministry preferences uniquely equip you for ministry.

The *Wired for Ministry* Personal Ministry Planning process will help you identify ministries that might be a good fit based on what you've learned. Summary sections in each inventory will prompt you to score your responses and record your top findings. In Step Three, you'll transfer your summary information to the correlating sections of your Personal Ministry Profile at the end of this workbook or the e-form available at the link below.

PERSONAL MINISTRY PLANNING TOOLS

		Workbook	Online
STEP ONE Your Background	What things are you good at?	Skills	www.EmpowerMinistry.org/skills
	What learning have you completed?	Education	Not available online
	What are your work, ministry & life experiences?	Experience	Not available online
STEP TWO Your Motivation	What spiritual gifts has God given you?	Spiritual Gifts	www.EmpowerMinistry.org/gifts
	How do you passionately pursue ministry?	Ministry Drives	www.EmpowerMinistry.org/drives
	What ministries do you prefer?	Ministry Preferences	www.EmpowerMinistry.org/pref
STEP THREE Your "Resume"	A summary of results from all six self-assessment inventories.	Personal Ministry Profile	www.empowerministry.org/PMP

Table 3. The comprehensive suite of self-assessment inventories and the Personal Ministry Profile available in this workbook and online.

The entire inventory suite is included in this workbook and can be completed and scored in a hardcopy format. Online link addresses are also provided if you prefer to complete the assessments online. Either method requires you to transfer summary information to your *Personal Ministry Profile* at the end of the workbook or the e-form.

The Self-Assessment Suite

SKILLS   EDUCATION   EXPERIENCE   SPIRITUAL GIFTS   MINISTRY DRIVES   MINISTRY PREFERENCES

What is a self-assessment? Is it a test of some sort? A self-assessment is not a test. It does not have a specific outcome in mind. It's a way to learn about yourself by gathering data that includes information about your values, interests, personality type, and aptitudes. Your goal will be to find ministries that are suitable based on the results. Of course, there are other factors that you will have to weigh when making a final decision about how to serve, but that will happen during the next step of the process—career exploration.

WHY DO FORMAL SELF ASSESSMENTS?

How much do you know about yourself? If you are like most people, you probably have to give a lot of thought to this question before you can answer it. You might know what your hobbies are and that you are (or aren't) a people person. You probably couldn't explain with ease what work-related values are important to you, and while you may know some things that you are good at, you may not have a complete list of all your aptitudes.

Even if you could provide a rundown of every one of your characteristics, there's a good chance you don't know how to use that information to help you find a career that is a good fit. Utilizing a variety of self-assessment tools will help you put together all the pieces of the puzzle. The *Wired for Ministry* self-assessment inventories will produce the information you need to make an informed decision about the direction you'll take in volunteering for personal ministry.

LET'S GET STARTED

Begin the Personal Ministry Planning Process by reading the introduction to the Skills Inventory on the next page. As you continue through the workbook, you'll summarize your findings at the end of each inventory and transfer them to the correlating section of your Personal Ministry Profile. Space is provided throughout the workbook for making personal notes.

SKILLS

You've Got Skills

Whenhat skills do you possess? Possessing skills is more than just knowing about things. Skill is possession knowledge as seen through experience. It includes the intuition that comes after being involved in something over time. Your skill set is a valuable asset for the kingdom of God. If all we had was knowledge, we would all be the same within a standard deviation. It's the skills gained from knowledge over time that is part of our uniqueness.

Each of us has hundreds of skills, many of which we take for granted. Many of the things you do well clearly align with the needs of secular charitable agencies, the church, or para-church organizations. But as you complete the inventory, you may not see a direct link between your skills and serving. You may ask yourself, "How can I use this in my ministry?" The question is legitimate. It's common to separate our skills into categories of professional and recreational or Christian, secular or sacred. Perhaps you've thought, "My office skills belong at work," or, "How can I use my mechanic skills in ministry?" The problem has not been that the skills are wrong, but rather we haven't been creative enough to utilize them effectively for the kingdom.

Many charities, churches, and ministries cannot afford to hire qualified people with your skills to accomplish what needs to be done. Often, they're left to function without the computer, accounting, or office expertise that most secular businesses need and employ. These organizations often have inadequate facilities, vehicles, and equipment simply because they lack the skills or manpower to improve their situation. Your time and skills would be a valuable gift to a charity, church or ministry that otherwise would have to pay for the service.

There are also those people who could improve their income and support their family better if they could acquire a skill that you or someone else in the church could pass on. This would be possible if, as Christians, we would reach out and share our skills through tutoring or mentoring programs. As we give of ourselves, we share the love of God. Needs-based evangelism has the potential to reach many with the love of God who would otherwise never darken the doorways of our church. As you consider all the various skills, abilities and expertise that you have, pray that God will show you how you can use them in a volunteer capacity.

SKILL INVENTORY

■ PART ONE: CAREER RELATED SKILLS ■

INSTRUCTIONS: Read the list of skills in each skill category below (pages 10-12). Check the skills you're interested in using.

ADMINISTRATION
General
- O Non-profit executive management
- O Office management
- O Clerical
- O Assist in mailings
- O Phone

Computer Skills
- O Word processing
- O Spreadsheets
- O Database management
- O Desktop publishing
- O PowerPoint
- O Other

Accounting
- O General ledger
- O Payroll
- O Profit & Loss
- O Budget
- O Other

Governance
- O Board member
- O Task committee
- O Legal advice
- O Budget expertise
- O Strategic planning
- O Other

COMPUTER TECHNOLOGY
- O Set up computer network
- O Computer repair
- O Web design
- O Create & maintain web site
- O Set up accounting/database
- O Set up computer learning center
- O Install software
- O Helpdesk
- O Computer training
- O Data extractions
- O Spreadsheets
- O Database management
- O Accounting
- O Client record management

RESOURCE DEVELOPMENT
General
- O Direct mail fundraising
- O Major gift solicitation
- O Grant research
- O Grant writing
- O Special event volunteer
- O Church representative
- O Corporate sponsorship
- O Underwrite fundraising event

Gifts-in-kind Donations
- O Food
- O Clothing
- O Building supplies
- O Office equipment
- O Vehicles
- O Other

MARKETING
Advertising
- O Copywriting
- O Creative art
- O Displays/ads
- O Radio commercials
- O Television commercials
- O Sponsorship
- O Cause marketing other

Publicity
- O Public Service Announcement
- O Press conference
- O Media kit
- O Press release
- O Other

BUILDINGS/GROUNDS/VEHICLES
- O Construction
- O Building maintenance
- O Vehicle maintenance
- O Electrical
- O Plumbing
- O Landscaping
- O Painting
- O Building Committee member
- O Help with clean up

JOB CREATION/TRAINING/READINESS
- O Mentor someone looking for employment
- O Temporary service agent
- O Assist someone laid off work
- O GED trainer
- O Guidance counselor
- O Career coach
- O Job trainer
- O Job retention specialist
- O Job advancement specialist
- O Conflict resolution
- O Counseling
- O Substance abuse counselor
- O Company employment liaison
- O Grant writer
- O Incubator management

EDUCATION
General
- O Provide performance for event
- O Teaching
- O Guidance counseling
- O Special education
- O Administration
- O Teaching skills trainer
- O Library/research skills
- O Organize and design curriculum
- O Recreation
- O Foodservice
- O Tutoring
- O English ESL
- O Reading
- O Math
- O Science
- O Other

MENTORING
- O Case management
- O Social skill trainer
- O Accountability partner
- O Strong listening skills
- O Coach
- O Appointment coordinator
- O Job trainer
- O Provide transportation

HUMAN RESOURCES
- O Interviewing skills
- O Personality assessment
- O Skills assessment
- O Personnel development
- O Conflict resolution
- O Career development
- O Other

SOUND/VIDEO/MEDIA
- O Assist with the sound system
- O Edit video
- O Storyboard videos
- O Run camera for video production
- O Run audio/visual
- O Set up PowerPoint presentations

VISUAL ARTS
- O Make signs
- O Use desktop publishing
- O Paint a mural
- O Photography
- O Illustrated literature
- O Interior design and decorating
- O Architecture
- O Crafts
- O Fine arts
- O Sculpture/clay

MUSIC
- O Compose songs
- O Play in orchestra
- O Sign in choir
- O Play in band
- O Lead singing
- O Arrange music
- O Play accompaniment for singers

DRAMA/SPEECH
- O Direct a play
- O Write skits
- O Speak in front of groups
- O Write a drama
- O Perform in a drama
- O Dramatic storytelling
- O Work as stagehand

EMERGENCY/DISASTER
- O Project manager
- O Medical personnel
- O Volunteer coordinator
- O Disaster clean-up volunteer
- O Assist with meals for the suffering
- O Collect food for the hungry
- O Find shelter for the needy
- O Caseworker

FAMILY SPECIALIST
General
- ○ Family finances
- ○ Asset building
- ○ Homemaker specialist

Parenting skills trainer
- ○ Infant
- ○ Toddler
- ○ Grade school
- ○ Teenager

CHILDREN WORKER
- ○ Assist with infants in nursery
- ○ Read stories to children
- ○ Help with pre-school
- ○ Teach crafts and games to children
- ○ Child day care specialist
- ○ Child day care assistant
- ○ Child day care administrator
- ○ Sunday school teacher

ELDERCARE
- ○ Take meals to shut-ins
- ○ Pick up elderly for special meetings
- ○ Comfort those who are sick
- ○ Visit elderly in nursing homes
- ○ Give respite to caretakers
- ○ Home health care
- ○ Medical specialist

HEALTH
- ○ Medical doctor
- ○ Physician assistant
- ○ Nurse
- ○ Dental professional
- ○ Other

ECONOMIC DEVELOPMENT
- ○ Tutor/mentor job skills
- ○ Mechanic
- ○ Auto body repair
- ○ Carpentry
- ○ Electrical
- ○ Plumbing
- ○ Cement
- ○ Masonry
- ○ Landscaping
- ○ Building maintenance
- ○ Carpet cleaning
- ○ Maid service
- ○ Truck driving
- ○ Retail sales

SOCIAL WORK
- ○ Social worker
- ○ Caseworker
- ○ Substance abuse counselor
- ○ Family and marriage counselor
- ○ Adoption/foster care
- ○ Eldercare
- ○ Special education

ADULT WORKER
- ○ train adult teachers
- ○ Lead single adult groups
- ○ Teach parenting skills
- ○ Organize marriage seminars
- ○ Organize men's/women's group
- ○ Adult counseling

YOUTH WORKER
- ○ Lead youth group
- ○ Plan youth activities
- ○ Spend time with youth on a retreat
- ○ Drive young people to events
- ○ Drug counselor
- ○ Youth guidance counselor
- ○ Chaperone youth retreat
- ○ Lead games on youth night
- ○ Counsel at youth camp
- ○ Lead/teach/coach sports
- ○ Sunday school teacher

HOUSING
- ○ Regional and neighborhood planning
- ○ General contracting
- ○ Carpentry
- ○ Electrical
- ○ Plumbing
- ○ Cement
- ○ Masonry
- ○ Landscaping
- ○ Alarm systems
- ○ Financing
- ○ Mortgage
- ○ Government programs
- ○ Foundation grants
- ○ Real estate sales
- ○ Real estate management
- ○ Rural housing
- ○ REIT

▧ PART TWO: OTHER SKILLS ▧

INSTRUCTIONS: List any skills acquired over your lifetime that are not already indicated in the skills inventory section.

SKILLS	SPORTS, HOBBIES & INTERESTS

▧ SKILL INVENTORY SUMMARY ▧

INSTRUCTIONS: Review Parts One and Two of the Skill Inventory and determine the top 5 skills that you'd like to use in a ministry or vocation. List them below. Transfer this summary information to your **Personal Ministry Profile** in the workbook or e-form.

TOP 5 SKILLS

1 _____
2 _____
3 _____
4 _____
5 _____

WIRED
for
MINISTRY

Your Education and Experience Matter

skills · **EDUCATION** · **EXPERIENCE** · spiritual gifts · ministry drives · ministry preferences

There are various ways that we, as individuals, learn. As you go through these inventories, please stop and consider the many ways that you've learned in your life. Ask yourself, "How can I use my knowledge and experiences in ministry?" If you're like most, you'll discover that the ministries you've participated in have often been more connected to your experiential and heart knowledge than your formal education.

Head Knowledge. The primary way we learn is through participation in the formal education system where we follow a progressive curriculum and, upon completion, receive accreditation. Secondary avenues of education provide opportunities for lifelong learning through training seminars, subject-specific conferences, internet courses, and on-the-job training. Together, they develop a reservoir of education often referred to as *head knowledge*.

Life Experience and Heart Knowledge. Simultaneously, we develop *experiential knowledge*. Life experiences from work, family, social, and civil contexts give us valuable knowledge that we don't receive from formal education. Much of this knowledge can be used in numerous ministries. Faith, hope, love, and trust in God are some of the areas that develop as we experience life with God. Finally, we all develop *heart knowledge*.

> "And if someone asks about your Christian hope, always be ready to explain it" (1 Peter 3:15, *New Living Translation*).

> "All praise to God, the Father of our Lord Jesus Christ. God is our merciful Father and the source of all comfort. He comforts us in all our troubles so that we can comfort others. When they are troubled, we will be able to give them the same comfort God has given us" (2 Corinthians 1:3-4).

Heart knowledge is developed as we, or someone we love, go through life's stressful situations. Life is full of hardships, but with God's help, we can minister to others going through similar circumstances. In ministry, this empathy is helpful in giving comfort, counseling, leading support. Heart knowledge produces the mental toughness, resilience, and patience that comes from having gone down one of life's difficult roads.

EDUCATION INVENTORY

▓ EDUCATIONAL HISTORY ▓

INSTRUCTIONS: Check each level of education you have completed, listing majors as applicable. List professional titles, certifications, and other training.

COMPLETED EDUCATION LEVELS

○	High School or GED	
○	Associate Degree	Major
○	Bachelor's Degree	Major
○	Master's Degree	Major
○	Doctorate	Major

PROFESSIONAL TITLES, CERTIFICATIONS, AND OTHER TRAINING

☐

▓ EDUCATION INVENTORY SUMMARY ▓

INSTRUCTIONS: Review the Education Inventory and determine the types of knowledge you've gained that could be used in a ministry or vocation. List them below. Transfer this summary information to your **Personal Ministry Profile** in the workbook or e-form.

KNOWLEDGE GAINED

EXPERIENCE INVENTORY

▓ PART ONE: CAREER AND VOLUNTEER EXPERIENCE ▓

INSTRUCTIONS FOR COMPLETING PART ONE: Record your work experience, military service, and volunteer experience.

CAREER EXPERIENCE
Work and Military

CURRENT / MOST RECENT WORK EXPERIENCE

Organization

Job Title

Responsibilities

SIGNIFICANT PRIOR WORK EXPERIENCE

Organization

Job Title

Responsibilities

MILITARY SERVICE

Branch

Rank

Countries Stationed

Responsibilities

VOLUNTEER EXPERIENCE
Non-profit Organizations, Civic Groups, Associations, and Social Clubs

Organization

City/State

Type of Work

Organization

City/State

Type of Work

Organization

City/State

Type of Work

▓ PART TWO: ACHIEVEMENTS ▓

INSTRUCTIONS FOR COMPLETING PART TWO: Record your significant achievements, awards, and honors.

ACHIEVEMENTS
Achievements, Awards, and Honors from Childhood, Young Adulthood, and Adulthood

Childhood

Young Adulthood

Adulthood

▓ PART THREE: LIFE SITUATION EXPERIENCE ▓

INSTRUCTIONS FOR COMPLETING PART THREE: Difficult situations occur in everyone's life. Read the list of situations below and check any that you or someone you know has gone through and in which you believe you could relate to others in that situation. Briefly describe your experience.

○ **Grief and Loss** (e.g. death, divorce, disaster, theft, assault, fraud)

○ **Health and Medical** (e.g. chronic conditions, disabilities, being a care provider)

○ **Finance** (e.g. poverty, job loss, bankruptcy, business failure, poor credit)

○ **Emotional** (e.g. depression, anxiety, anger, sadness, uncertainty)

○ **Relationships** (e.g. marriage, in-laws, parenting, siblings, work, adapting socially)

▧ EXPERIENCE INVENTORY SUMMARY ▧

INSTRUCTIONS: Review Parts One, Two, and Three of the Experience Inventory (pages 17-18) and determine the experience you've gained that could be used in a ministry or vocation. List them below. Transfer this summary information to your **Personal Ministry Profile** in the workbook or e-form.

EXPERIENCE GAINED

SPIRITUAL GIFTS

God Gives Spiritual Gifts and Equipping Roles

skills   education   experience   **SPIRITUAL GIFTS**   ministry drives   ministry preferences

In this section, you'll review the various gifts that God has given to the church and to us as individual believers and consider how each applies to you. A spiritual gift is an ability or prompting of the Holy Spirit, given to us freely and energized and empowered by God for his service. The list of spiritual gifts Paul provided includes administration, discernment, encouragement, faith, giving, healing, helping, teaching, leadership, knowledge, mercy, miracles, prophecy, service, and wisdom. Paul also wrote that God also gave some people the role of pastor, evangelist, teacher, apostle, and prophet.

The three-part Spiritual Gift Inventory considers the *spiritual gifts* and *equipping roles* that God has given to you to perform a variety of ministry functions that utilize service gifts. The emphasis is on the call of God which includes the passion, abilities, spiritual gifts, and experience that God has given you.

- **Part One: Ministry Tasks.** Part One describes various *ministry tasks* associated with each spiritual gift. These tasks are divided into five sections. Each section includes one beginning phrase followed by a list of fifteen different ending phrases. When read together, the beginning phrase followed by each ending phrase forms a sentence that correlates to one of the spiritual gifts. You'll rate each spiritual gift based on how the ministry tasks associated with them apply to you.

- **Part Two: Service Opportunity Descriptions.** Part Two describes various service opportunities associated with each spiritual gift. The description for each spiritual gift includes a definition, benefits, pitfalls, service opportunities, and further training. You'll rate each spiritual gift based on your passion for and experience with the service opportunities associated with it.

27

- **Part Three: Equipping Roles.** Part Three describes various responsibilities associated with each equipping role. The description for each equipping role includes a definition, responsibilities, and training and qualifications. You'll rate each equipping role based on your passion for and experience with serving in these roles.

SPIRITUAL GIFT INVENTORY

▦ PART ONE: MINISTRY TASKS ▦

INSTRUCTIONS FOR COMPLETING PART ONE: There are five sections in Part One (pages 22-24). Each section includes one beginning phrase at the top of the section box and a list of fifteen ending phrases listed below it. Complete sentences are created by reading the beginning phrase followed by each ending phrase. Each complete sentence correlates to one of the fifteen spiritual gifts. Begin in Section 1 by reading the beginning phrase ("I have volunteered to...") followed by the first ending phrase ("...do menial projects that need to be done"). Think about the sentence and rate how it applies to you using the rating scale below. Use the same procedure to rate each of the ending phrases in all five sections.

RATING SCALE: 0-3 (0 = almost never | 1 = sometimes | 2 = often | 3 = almost always)

SECTION 1: I have volunteered to . . .

\newline RATING 0	1	2	3		SPIRITUAL GIFT
○	○	○	○	do menial projects that need to be done.	14
○	○	○	○	speak out against immorality.	13
○	○	○	○	step out in faith, trust God for the supernatural.	12
○	○	○	○	help those in need.	11
○	○	○	○	be involved in decision-making process.	9
○	○	○	○	assist person to learn Bible.	8
○	○	○	○	help behind the scenes.	7
○	○	○	○	pray for people to be healed and it happened.	6
○	○	○	○	give to a cause.	5
○	○	○	○	step out in faith and go for it.	4
○	○	○	○	teach godly living from the Bible.	15
○	○	○	○	urge people to live for Christ.	3
○	○	○	○	do research on biblical topics.	10
○	○	○	○	help find the truth in a situation.	2
○	○	○	○	organize tasks in order to reach a goal.	1

SECTION 2: God has enabled me to . . .

\newline RATING 0	1	2	3		SPIRITUAL GIFT
○	○	○	○	discern between good and evil.	2
○	○	○	○	create strategies to reach a goal.	1
○	○	○	○	comfort people from God's Word.	3
○	○	○	○	believe him for great things.	4
○	○	○	○	apply the Bible to everyday problems.	15
○	○	○	○	share my resources.	5
○	○	○	○	keep the church going by serving where needed.	7
○	○	○	○	stand up for what is right according to his Word.	13
○	○	○	○	teach a Sunday School class.	8
○	○	○	○	study and understand biblical issues.	10
○	○	○	○	perceive clear direction in specific circumstances.	9
○	○	○	○	pray and the result has sometimes been healing.	6
○	○	○	○	assist those that cannot help themselves.	11
○	○	○	○	pray for God to perform supernaturally and it happened.	12
○	○	○	○	help set up for programs in the church.	14

SECTION 3: People ask me to . . .

RATING 0	1	2	3		SPIRITUAL GIFT
○	○	○	○	tell them if a teaching is true or false.	2
○	○	○	○	pray to God for mighty things.	4
○	○	○	○	do the jobs others don't want to do.	14
○	○	○	○	lead a project.	1
○	○	○	○	help someone in need.	7
○	○	○	○	explain the scriptures regarding a problem they are having.	15
○	○	○	○	give oversight to a program or process.	9
○	○	○	○	pray for them during an illness.	6
○	○	○	○	bring encouragement to someone.	3
○	○	○	○	help them understand deep spiritual truths.	10
○	○	○	○	share with others in need.	5
○	○	○	○	pray that God will intervene supernaturally.	12
○	○	○	○	teach a class.	8
○	○	○	○	show compassion to someone hurting.	11
○	○	○	○	lead the fight against evil in our community.	13

SECTION 4: I am burdened to . . .

RATING 0	1	2	3		SPIRITUAL GIFT
○	○	○	○	coordinate people, ideas and resources to reach a goal.	1
○	○	○	○	trust God for great things.	4
○	○	○	○	do behind-the-scene jobs to get ministry done.	14
○	○	○	○	pray for those that are hurting.	6
○	○	○	○	help and support where I can.	7
○	○	○	○	make sure that ministry(s) keep focused and on task.	9
○	○	○	○	help people understand biblical truth.	10
○	○	○	○	prevent false doctrine or confusion from spreading.	2
○	○	○	○	organize to help the poor and needy.	11
○	○	○	○	use the scriptures in counseling others.	15
○	○	○	○	lead people to believe in God's almighty power.	12
○	○	○	○	give happily to different needs.	5
○	○	○	○	help with Christian education.	8
○	○	○	○	make sure we are pure in our walk with God.	13
○	○	○	○	challenge people to live the life God wants them to.	3

RATING 0	1	2	3		SPIRITUAL GIFT
O	O	O	O	pray about serious issues.	4
O	O	O	O	do jobs that I know others might not volunteer for.	14
O	O	O	O	organize activities.	1
O	O	O	O	pray for seemingly impossible situations & God performs it.	12
O	O	O	O	comfort people who are hurting.	11
O	O	O	O	stimulate people spiritually.	3
O	O	O	O	give to different needs in the church.	5
O	O	O	O	study more about biblical truth.	10
O	O	O	O	teach where I am needed.	8
O	O	O	O	help distinguish if something is right or wrong.	2
O	O	O	O	help guide and direct a ministry(s).	9
O	O	O	O	listen to people's hurts & pray for God to heal them.	6
O	O	O	O	teach biblical truths about living.	15
O	O	O	O	speak up against ungodliness.	13
O	O	O	O	give people assistance.	7

▣ SPIRITUAL GIFT PART ONE: SCORING ▣

PART ONE SCORING INSTRUCTIONS: Each section in Part One includes fifteen complete sentences created by reading the beginning phrase followed by each ending phrase. Each sentence correlates to one of the fifteen spiritual gifts, as listed in the scoring chart below. Begin in Section 1 by scanning down through the *Spiritual Gift* column to locate the number "1." Transfer your rating for that sentence to the scoring chart below next to *"1 – Administration."*

EXAMPLE: If you rated yourself as a "2" for the first complete sentence in Section 1, record it as shown below.

	SPIRITUAL GIFT	SECTION 1	SECTION 2	SECTION 3	SECTION 4	SECTION 5	TOTAL
1	Administration	2					

Continue through each section in Part One, transferring your ratings for sentences designated as "1" in the corresponding columns next to *Administration* in the scoring chart below. Use the same procedure for each spiritual gift number until all ratings have been transferred and totaled. Add the numbers together horizontally for each spiritual gift and write the sum in the *Total* column. The most points you can have for each spiritual gift is fifteen.

	SPIRITUAL GIFT	SECTION 1	SECTION 2	SECTION 3	SECTION 4	SECTION 5	TOTAL
1	Administration						
2	Discernment						
3	Encouragement						
4	Faith						
5	Giving						
6	Healing						
7	Helping						
8	Teaching						
9	Leadership						
10	Knowledge						
11	Mercy						
12	Miracles						
13	Prophecy						
14	Service						
15	Wisdom						

UNDERSTANDING YOUR SCORE: Your rating scores indicate the way you see God using you in various ministry situations. Review the score ranges below to interpret and understand your scores in the scoring chart on the previous page. Remember, there is a difference between a passion or talent and a spiritual gift. You can find out more about this by reading our book, *How to Use Your Spiritual Gifts.*

- You may be a good teacher, but has God given you the spiritual gift of teaching for him?
- You may be passionate about mercy in a particular area, but has God burdened you to be merciful in a ministry for him?
- You can be a leader at work, but has God's anointing caused you to use leadership in ministry?
- You can be very discerning about many things, but has God directed you to be discerning in matters of church or scripture?

The highest number of points available for each spiritual gift is fifteen. These scores represent the way God has used you in various ministry situations.

15-13: Dominant Preference. If you're not already involved in using this gift, you should consider it. We recommend that you meet with a spiritual leader and ask them to confirm that this is, indeed, a spiritual gift God has given you. Let your pastor know about this gift and ask for specific ways you can use it for service.

12-10: Strong Preference. You have a strong desire to be involved using this gift. Talk to your pastor or get input from other church leaders. If you need more experience, ask others in the church to pray for you about this gift. If you aren't aware of service opportunities, research ways this gift can be used to serve.

9-8: Moderate Preference. You have some interest, so if you think or feel God wants you to explore it further, get some input from your pastor. Because you have some level of preference or experience with this gift, it's likely that you'll occasionally be called on to use it, so invest some time in learning more about this gift.

7-below: We have been purposeful in writing questions that indicate the use of these gifts for the spiritual direction of the church. Perhaps those questions caused your lower score. You can be strong in this attribute and yet not exercise it in ministry or church matters. If you think or feel your score does not indicate your true spiritual gifting, go to the definitions section in our How to Use Your Spiritual Gifts book for more explanation. We all are called upon from time to time to be involved in many of the Christian virtues of mercy, wisdom, helping, and faith. These are part of our Christian maturity. If after you explore this further and believe it is your gift, we encourage you to pursue it under the Lord's direction.

■ SPIRITUAL GIFT PART ONE: SUMMARY ■

INSTRUCTIONS: In Part One, you rated each spiritual gift based on how the ministry tasks associated with them relate to you. Review the rating totals column in the scoring chart on Page 24 and determine your top spiritual gifts. List them below.

PART ONE: MINISTRY TASKS

_____

_____

_____

_____

INSTRUCTIONS FOR COMPLETING PART TWO: Part Two (pages 26-40) includes service opportunity descriptions for each of the fifteen spiritual gifts. Read the service opportunity description for each spiritual gift and rate yourself in both *passion* and *experience* using the rating scale below. Space is provided for making any personal notes that come to mind as you complete Part Two.

RATING SCALE: 1-5 (1 = low | 2 = somewhat low | 3 = moderate | 4 = somewhat high | 5 = high)

- **Passion.** How motivated are you to take action in this way?
- **Experience.** How much experience do you have with this type of service? How much evidence is there of this gift in your life?

1. ADMINISTRATION

Definition. In I Corinthians 12:28, it says, "Then gifts of healing, helping, administrating" (NEV). In the biblical language, the word *administration* was a unique term that meant "to govern, pilot, direct, or steer." It was used to describe a person steering a ship, variations of which appear in the New Testament describing life on the Mediterranean Sea. A person with the gift of administration is a good strategic thinker, organized, has supervisory skills, and manages people and projects well. When directions are set by leadership, a person with this gift can help accomplish the job efficiently.

Benefits. The gift of administration can help leadership accomplish great things. Good administration can save time and money. In a volunteer situation, the gift of administration can bring professional skills to many events, meetings, and projects. When directions are set by leadership, this person can help accomplish the job efficiently and help meet strategic goals.

Pitfalls. It is easy for a person with the gift of administration to become so involved in a project that they become insensitive to the needs of others. It may be hard to understand why others may not have the same passion for details or organization. Some people with this gift can use their position to bully people or exhibit a my-way-or-the-highway attitude. Some may be tempted to take on too much work and personal responsibilities, leading to troubles in other parts of their life. There may be over dependency on the gift, so God is organized out of the project.

Service Opportunities. A person with this gift can help start and administer events, organize meetings, help with finances, schedule meetings, and assist in office administration. This gift can be used in Sunday School or Christian education supervision. When the pastor or church leaders have a project, a person with this gift can help accomplish it. Many para-church ministries need help with their administration.

Further Training. To help grow the gift of administration, they could take management courses and become proficient in computer skills. This person could volunteer on small projects or be mentored by an experienced person with this gift.

Passion Rating:		1-5 (1 = low; 5 = high)
Experience Rating:		

NOTES

_____

_____

_____

_____

Definition. In I Corinthians 12:10, it says, "He gives someone else the ability to discern whether a message is from the Spirit of God or from another spirit." In the biblical language, the word *discernment* meant "to be able to distinguish between right and wrong, good and evil." It involves possessing a logical, judicial ability to think through issues. It is the ability to determine if a saying, teaching, doctrine, written word, or event is good or evil, true or false; and if the source, meaning, or intentions are of God, the individual person, or satanic deception. People with this gift have an ability to read between the lines and find the truth of an issue. This is often a gut reaction that signifies when something doesn't seem to be right, along with an urgency to pray and ask for wisdom.

Benefits. Ministry can be messy. We see this in the Bible. Whenever there are people involved, there are many different opportunities for miscommunication, hidden agendas, and emotional issues. Spiritual battle, whether in a small group or the church, is a serious concern and the gift of discernment is a valuable asset to have. A person with the gift of discernment can work with leadership in keeping things in check. This gift can help guide the church both in more ordinary decisions or deeper spiritual issues.

Pitfalls. There is a temptation for a person with this gift to always be right, to not admit when there has been a mistake. The need to be right may outweigh the desire for truth. Pride could prevent a humble spirit in the use of this gift. It could be tempting for this person to misuse the trust that someone places in their judgment and use the gift for personal gain or to hurt someone. It is easy for a person with the gift of discernment to think they are the source of discernment, trusting in their own personal judgment and not consulting God, thus being self-deceived.

Service Opportunities. This gift can be used to settle disputes or in counseling, spiritual warfare, or assisting church leadership with decisions. It can be used in counseling with addictions and low self-esteem where deception is sometimes used as a coping mechanism.

Further Training. Good biblical training is key for people with the gift of discernment. Prayer and spiritual warfare are two excellent subjects for a person with this gift to study. Listening skills are very important. If possible, they should find someone else with this gift that will mentor them.

Passion Rating:	
Experience Rating:	

1-5 (1 = low; 5 = high)

NOTES

_____

_____

_____

_____

_____

_____

_____

_____

_____

_____

Definition. In Romans 12:8, it says, "If your gift is to encourage others, be encouraging." The biblical meaning of the word *encouragement* is "to call someone near to console, comfort, exhort, implore with them." Although the goal of this gift is to comfort, motivate and give a reason for hope, there is also an important element of exhortation that points to the future. A person with the gift of encouragement is moved when they see someone down and likes to comfort and motivate them toward change, encouraging the believer to be what God wants them to be. They share hope for the future. The nature of this gift is like dispensing medicine; a singular action used in the moment to bring about a long-term effect.

Benefits. This gift helps with morale, motivating people toward action, and making people feel that they are part of a group. This is an important part of love-in-action and is often the most memorable part of ministry to hurting people.

Pitfalls. People with the gift of encouragement may be tempted to take care of needs by giving quick-fixes without truly listening to the underlying problems. A person with this gift can end up giving pat answers in the form of spiritual jargon and formulas instead of the empathy and caring required. There is a danger in enabling the person in need rather than helping them. For someone with this gift, encouragement could become more about their need to be an encourager than the person's need to be helped. When the focus is on the needs of the encourager, real spiritual solutions can be missed.

Service Opportunities. This gift can be used in making people feel welcome and a part of the church. It can also be used in ministries for single parents, those that are sick, or problems associated with being elderly. This gift can be used in small group interaction, counseling, home visitation, or personal mentoring. Meals for those in crisis, Stephen ministers, and lay chaplains can be ministries where this gift is used.

Further Training. Biblical and/or pastoral counseling and psychology courses would help a person with this gift understand the dynamics of this gift. To help grow the gift or encouragement, lessons in effective listening, crisis counseling, empathy, and caregiving would be helpful.

Passion Rating:		1-5 (1 = low; 5 = high)
Experience Rating:		

NOTES

_____
_____
_____
_____
_____
_____
_____
_____
_____
_____

Definition. In I Corinthians 12:9 it says, "And to another faith by the same Spirit" (NIV). In the biblical language, the word *faith* meant "persuasion, credence or moral conviction." It is an assurance and belief. The gift of faith involves a prompting from God to trust him for the supernatural; to continue even when there are difficult circumstances. A person with this gift is fully persuaded that God has the ability to answer prayer and work everything according to his will. When this person learns about certain situations that seem impossible, God seems to nudge them to trust him. This nudge is more than a quiet trust; it is open, stepping out affirmation of God in the situation. God gives this person a sense of assurance in his ability and desire to work in the situation. As a result, they are free to ask God for his intervention without usurping God's sovereignty.

Benefits. The gift of faith encourages the congregation, gives hope to believers and is a witness to unbelievers. This gift instills confidence in God's ability to help individuals and the church reach the vision God has for them.

Pitfalls. There is a danger for people with this gift in becoming despondent, depressed or angry when answers don't go their way. Satan uses disappointment to challenge believers' faith and it is easy for a person with the gift of faith to become critical of those who are doubting. It may also be possible for this person to believe that every situation calls for their response and, in doing so, become overstressed. It is best to seek God's will and ask him how to pray in the situation. This person can falsely think that it is their faith that is doing mighty things. This can lead to arrogance and pride. Instead, they must remember it is God who does mighty works; they must remain dependent on him and his leading. It is God who answers prayer and he must get the glory. There is a temptation for this person to think that faith is the end in and of itself. It is not. A person with this gift needs to pray for discernment and exercise their faith toward God's true will in the situation.

Service Opportunities. This gift can be used in making people feel welcome and a part of the church. It can also be used in ministries for single parents, those that are sick or problems associated with being elderly. This gift can be used in small group interaction, counseling, home visitation or personal mentoring. Meals for those in crisis, Stephen ministers, and lay chaplains can be ministries where this gift is used.

Further Training. Biblical and/or pastoral counseling and psychology courses would help a person with this gift understand the dynamics of this gift. To help grow the gift or encouragement, lessons in effective listening, crisis counseling, empathy, and caregiving would be helpful.

Passion Rating:		1-5 (1 = low; 5 = high)
Experience Rating:		

NOTES

_____

_____

_____

_____

_____

_____

_____

5. GIVING

Definition. In Romans 12:8, it says, "If it is giving, give generously." In the biblical language, the word *giving* meant "to impart, to give over, share, bestow, bring forth, commit, deliver or grant." As a spiritual gift, giving is more than just casually giving something to someone. It implies the giving of yourself with the gift and can include giving your time, abilities, knowledge, love and resources to the cause of Christ. Like a pianist accompanies a soloist, a person with this gift enhances the giving. Together they are God's melody to the person receiving. Paul's exhortation implies that we should give generously with contentment and a cheerful attitude. When a person with this gift sees certain needs, God's Spirit nudges them in a way that they feel compelled to give what is needed in the situation as an agent of God's grace and mercy.

Benefits. The gift of giving helps teach grace and encourages faith in God. Obedience to this gift allows God to bring about the resources to accomplish his will for the church.

Pitfalls. A person with this gift must avoid the pharisaical trap of giving into the temptations of praise and pride by making sure others know about their generous deeds. It may be easy for this person to become critical and judge others that don't give in the same way they do. It is also possible for them to feel that they need to earn God's love, or they may have a deep need for praise and recognition. This can result in an inordinate amount of time or resources being given away, sometimes to the extent that family needs are ignored. Sometimes a person with the gift of giving experiences burnout or compassion fatigue. A common concern for people with this gift is enabling someone instead of helping them be responsible or giving money to projects that continue dependency rather than solving the root problems.

Service Opportunities. A person with the gift of giving often has expertise in money matters and can help with church finances and motivate others to give because of their example. They should be aware of the plans of the church, so they can be the best steward of what God has given them. They can also pray and help the church with outreach that would otherwise not be in the budget. This person can be an effective mentor to other people with resources in the church.

Further Training. A person with the gift of giving does not automatically get wisdom with it. There needs to be due diligence on prospective recipients of their generosity. The study of philanthropy and various financial giving vehicles will help a person with this gift leverage their generosity effectively. Reading biographies of businesspeople who were generous, as well as stories of missionaries and ministries and how God called many to respond to needs, will be inspiring.

Passion Rating:		1-5 (1 = low; 5 = high)
Experience Rating:		

NOTES

Definition. In I Corinthians 12 it says, "And to someone else the one Spirit gives the gift of healing." In the biblical language, the word *healing* meant 'to affect a cure through God's supernatural power.' This gift is similar to faith. When a person with the gift of healing learns about situations that need healing—physical, emotional, or spiritual—God leads them to step out, affirm him, and believe him for healing. God gives them assurance in his ability and desire to work in the situation. A person with this gift feels free to ask God for his intervention without usurping his sovereignty. There is a deep understanding that they do not have the personal power to heal anyone, but they've been given a great conviction to pray for healing and to believe in God's power. This gift is used when God ordains and for his glory.

Benefits. This gift encourages faith and hope in the local church. Healing can spark revival, repentance, encourage those new in the faith, and ultimately leads to God's glory. God often used this as a sign to unbelievers.

Pitfalls. There is a temptation to hero-worship a person with the gift of healing. This puts an expectancy on the person to perform, sometimes without seeking God's will in the matter. Pride can also be a problem, causing someone with this gift to exaggerate, make false claims, or worry about their reputation. There is potential jealousy over others with the gift. There can be disappointment, anger, bitterness or future fear of failure for this person when God does not answer in the way they think that he should. When healing does not take effect, a person with this gift needs to be careful about judging someone for lack of faith or sin in their life. There is also the temptation to acquire riches by using the gift of healing.

Service Opportunities. This gift could be used on a prayer team, in a visitation ministry to the sick and elderly, or as part of a need-based evangelism program. A person with this gift is often called to a private prayer life for those that they know are sick and hurting physically and emotionally.

Further Training. Keeping a journal will help a person with the gift of healing stay focused and trust God when situations are difficult. Meeting with others who have this gift will be beneficial. Reading the scriptures is good for this person's personal encouragement and faith. To grow this gift, read biographies of men and women that God has used in this way or take training on the subject.

Passion Rating:		1-5 (1 = low; 5 = high)
Experience Rating:		

NOTES

_____

_____

_____

_____

_____

_____

_____

_____

_____

Definition. In I Corinthians 12, it says "A spiritual gift is given to each of us so we can help each other." The gift of helping is different than just the passive help associated with service or being a servant. The biblical meaning of the word *help* is an involvement that goes deeper than just serving someone. There are three parts to the biblical meaning of helping: 1) "bringing relief or giving assistance," 2) "taking hold of something or to support and to participate with someone," which requires involvement on the part of the person helping and sharing with others deeply. This is more than serving; it is deep, personal support. It literally means to "grab them, strongly lay hold of, to hold them up," and 3) "to exchange." This infers an exchange between a person with this gift and the person being helped. A person with the gift of helping sees the needy as a giver, not just a receiver, and they get blessed, too.

Benefits. In the early church, helping others resulted in many coming to know the Lord. This can be part of a needs-based evangelism program. This gift will help the overall witness of the church and can also be used to help those in the church. The gift of helping is part of fulfilling God's command to love one another.

Pitfalls. It is easy for a person with this gift to feel that they are the only one helping. A person can become discouraged, or, worse, bitter at others that are not helping. It can be hard to say "no" and easy to be taken advantage of. This person can fall victim to a subtle belief in work-based salvation, even though they know they are saved by grace. If this person is not careful, they can burn out from compassion fatigue. Because of the gratitude of people receiving help and the adulation from those that notice their work, a person with the gift of helping can become proud and fall into temptations that come along with pride. They need to make sure they don't enable others by creating dependency upon the help they provide. Instead, this person should focus on helping others develop the ability to help themselves.

Service Opportunities. This gift is a good way for new people to get involved in ministry. A person with this gift can be part of a mentoring program and would also be a good fit in visitation/ministry for the sick, elderly, single parents, and underprivileged youth and families.

Further Training. Training in people skills, basic counseling, listening, empathy, and cross-cultural ministry would help grow this gift. Specialty training in areas of passion is useful for specific ministries. Devotional reading on mercy ministries would be inspirational. Spiritual warfare training would benefit a person with this gift, so they can understand and address spiritual bondage issues that arise.

Passion Rating:		1-5 (1 = low; 5 = high)
Experience Rating:		

NOTES

Definition. In Romans 12, it says, "If you are a teacher, teach well." In the biblical language, the word *teaching* meant "to communicate in a way that those hearing it can put it into practice." Teaching makes difficult truths understandable over time; it is instruction with the goal of the pupil retaining and applying what they learn to their own situations. A person with the gift of teaching has excitement in sharing the truth with other people and enjoys seeing people come alive when they get understanding. Someone with this gift may teach scripture and its interpretation and application or topical teaching that applies biblical truth to various topics. This person has a burden to share the Word of God and help people apply it to their own situations.

Benefits. Good teaching allows the church to equip the congregation for service. A person with this gift has the knowledge to accurately teach scriptures, which is used to instruct, reprove, correct, and train (1 Timothy 3:16). The gift of teaching helps Christians grow in their faith and reach out to others in the community.

Pitfalls. There can be a temptation for a person with this gift to rely on their own research, writing, and delivery skills rather than on the guidance of the Holy Spirit. Scripture warns us about the dangers of wanting praise. It can cause someone with this gift to teach what people want to hear instead of the truth, which may not be as popular. Pride may tempt this person to create their own following, judge those that do not enjoy studying or become legalistic or overly dogmatic.

Service Opportunities. This gift can be used in Sunday school or small group programs. With specialized knowledge, people with the gift of teaching can conduct seminars or special training classes. A person with this gift could teach in secular or Christian schools and could be used as a mentor in their field of expertise. This person could grow this gift by serving on the church's Christian education committee.

Further Training. For teaching the Bible, a person with this gift could take Bible courses or enroll in a Bible college or seminary degree program. To grow general teaching skills, this person could take classes to develop enhanced teaching and facilitation skills or find someone else with this gift that will mentor them. Learning about new technology and contemporary teaching methods will help grow the gift of teaching.

Passion Rating:		1-5 (1 = low; 5 = high)
Experience Rating:		

NOTES

_____
_____
_____
_____
_____
_____
_____
_____
_____

Definition. In Romans 12:8, it says, "If God has given you leadership ability, take the responsibility seriously." The biblical meaning of the word *leadership* is to "rule, preside, or stand over." A person with this gift is a visionary and gives direction and oversight to an organization. Whereas the person with the gift of administration steers the boat, the person with the gift of leadership is the captain and tells the person at the helm where to steer. This person has a deep conviction about a need and can see the solution; they are able to communicate why and when things need to be done.

Benefits. A church reaches goals when it has gifted leaders who are able to get things done. Like the conductor of an orchestra, a person with the gift of leadership will make use of all of the other gifts in the church and guide them into working in harmony. This gift is used to help the congregation reach maturity in Christ, evangelize the community, or reach out to those in need.

Pitfalls. Often, with leadership comes power and prestige. This can tempt a person with this gift to be overcome with pride and exaggerate their own importance, which can also create rivalry and jealousy. A person with the gift of leadership can be so goal- or vision-oriented that they run over people that get in the way or do not have the same passion for getting things done. It is easy for this person to dismiss, or worse, ridicule someone who disagrees with their point of view. A person with this gift can get discouraged and want to give up when things don't work out the way they envision. It is also easy for them to become over-involved in urgent matters and let other important issues like family, personal time, and devotion to God suffer.

Service Opportunities. This gift can be used to serve as a pastor, an elder, teacher, on a board, or in the governance of the church. Para-church organizations are always in need of good leaders.

Further Training. To grow the gift of leadership, consider professional development training. This could include leadership seminars/conferences, management courses, Bible and theology courses, and biblical teachings on discernment, wisdom, and character. Learning about vision, mission, goal setting, and how to develop and maintain effective teams is critical to good leadership. An earnest study of the Fruit of the Spirit would be a primer on the good qualities of a leader. A person with this gift could participate in a mentoring program, both as mentor and mentee, to deepen knowledge and experience.

Passion Rating:	
Experience Rating:	

1-5 (1 = low; 5 = high)

NOTES

_____

_____

_____

_____

_____

_____

_____

_____

10. KNOWLEDGE

Definition. In I Corinthians 12, it says, "To another the same Spirit gives a message of special knowledge." The biblical meaning of the word *knowledge* is "to know something experientially, intuitively and in the present." In this case, spiritual knowledge comes from God and is revealed through the Holy Spirit. A person with this gift is cognitively impressed with relevant insight that applies to a situation at hand. This is not a trance or channeling; the person relies on God to speak to them as a result of their experience with him and through his Word. The gift of knowledge is giving out what a person has learned and experienced. It could be an insight or a relevant message. A person with this gift desires to seek out, investigate, and personally experience the meaning of God's Word and then provide the insight they receive to help the church and others develop a relationship with Christ. The gift of knowledge is a Spirit-given ability to understand, in an exceptional way, what God wants to communicate in the moment.

Benefits. This gift is used to take God's Word and make truth relevant to specific situations in the church. In this way, God is able to speak to the believers in each generation and in each church.

Pitfalls. A person with the gift of knowledge can become prideful, overbearing, and insensitive to other people's opinions. Paul says, "if I understood all of God's secret plans and possessed all knowledge...but didn't love others, I would be nothing" (1 Corinthians 13:2). This person must also be careful of heresy or false teaching, ensuring that everything they share matches up with God's Word.

Service Opportunities. To grow this gift, this person should participate in opportunities that allow them to act on the knowledge and insight acquired through their relationship with God. This could include: teaching in the church or in a college/seminary setting, conducting seminars, writing educational materials, and speaking at learning events. This gift could also be used by leaders and trained counselors to edify others and make the Word relevant in others' lives.

Further Training. A person with the gift of knowledge should spend time in prayer and Bible study. There also must be a strong desire to know God and set aside time to hear from him. They could listen to teaching and preaching messages, enroll in Bible college or seminary courses and attend conferences that will deepen their knowledge. This person could participate in a mentoring program, both as mentor and mentee, to deepen their own knowledge and experience as well as those they mentor.

Passion Rating:		1-5 (1 = low; 5 = high)
Experience Rating:		

NOTES

_____

_____

_____

_____

_____

_____

_____

_____

_____

Definition. In Romans 12, Paul writes, "And if you have a gift for showing kindness to others, do it gladly." In the biblical language, the word *mercy* meant "to be led by God to be compassionate in your attitudes, words, and actions." It is more than sympathy, which is merely pity. Mercy is love in action. Empathy stirs deep inside a person with this gift and causes them to want to bring relief to the immediate physical, emotional, financial, or spiritual needs that they are aware of.

Benefits. A church that is merciful can help meet serious needs in the local community and also be an effective part of ministry within the congregation. Mercy helps relate the love of God to those in need and can be complemented with needs-based evangelism.

Pitfalls. Mercy can often give the impression that it is solving a problem when it may be only treating the immediate situation. By focusing on alleviating the symptoms, a person with the gift of mercy could miss the opportunity to really change the person and situation. Constantly rescuing people can enable them to remain helpless. Mercy is desperately needed, but this person must also strive for long-term solutions. It's possible for this person to get frustrated with others that don't get involved or don't see the problem and may become hurt or angry if they're taken for granted of or do not see the needed change. A person with this gift can be tempted to become over-involved, leading to burnout or too much time away from their family. It is also possible for this person to become proud of their mercy and become pharisaical, taking the attention and glory away from God.

Service Opportunities. The gift of mercy is a critical part of visitation programs, such as sick, elderly and prison ministries, homeless shelters, job placement programs, and food pantries. This gift can be used on boards and committees to help organizations be merciful. A person with this gift could volunteer for fundraising, mentoring, and counseling.

Further Training. To grow the gift of mercy, this person could consider taking seminars and reading books or articles about others with this gift in action. Volunteering will help grow this gift. College courses in the fields of social services, psychology, ministry, health, medicine, and education could lead to a career in a mercy ministry.

Passion Rating:		1-5 (1 = low; 5 = high)
Experience Rating:		

NOTES

_____
_____
_____
_____
_____
_____
_____
_____

Definition. In I Corinthians 12, Paul writes, "He gives one person the power to perform miracles." The biblical meaning of the term *miracle* is "a force or power; specifically, miraculous power." Like the gift of healing, the gift of miracles involves God's supernatural power. A person with this gift has a deep sensitivity to God's will in a situation and a deep belief in God's ability to fulfill it. They know where man's ability ends and God's supernatural power takes over. They have a spiritual burden to trust God in these situations and ask him to display his power for his glory. If the power of God were to be absent from the church, would we still function? How much do we really depend upon his power? We need to believe in God for the supernatural.

Benefits. God uses people in the church that have this gift to ask for his favor and blessings on the church. When difficulties come to the church and there seems no natural solution is available, God calls people with this gift to pray and trust him so that his glory may inspire the rest of the believers. The result is a healthy church, trusting and praising God for great things.

Pitfalls. Asking God to use his supernatural power can raise many temptations. Like Moses, a person with this gift can be tempted to step out on their own to perform a miracle. Or, like various biblical prophets, they may become bitter with disappointment if God doesn't answer the way they think he should. This person should be careful of pride, exaggeration, and false claims. They may become impatient, take the credit, suffer deep disappointment, or be tempted to create personal gain.

Service Opportunities. This gift gives support to pastors by praying for God's intervention and power to be manifested in the special needs of the church, congregation and surrounding community. The results will be God's mighty works as encouragement to the believers and signs and wonders to those that don't believe. This can help create an atmosphere of worship, praise, and holiness.

Further Training. A person with this gift needs to be a student of the Bible to encourage their faith. They need to examine how God has used this gift throughout biblical history. This gift can be grown by listening to sermons and teaching on this subject and by attending training classes. Reading biographies of people with this gift or stories of how this gift has been used in ministries will be inspiring for a person with this gift. If possible, they should find someone else with this gift that will mentor them. They should spend time in prayer and meditation with God, getting to know his heart so they can listen to his voice.

Passion Rating:		1-5 (1 = low; 5 = high)
Experience Rating:		

NOTES

_____

_____

_____

_____

_____

_____

_____

Definition. In Romans 12, Paul writes, "So if God has given you the ability to prophesy, speak out with as much faith as God has given you." The biblical meaning of *prophecy* is "a prediction (scriptural or other), an inspired speaker; or to speak under inspiration." In the Old Testament, prophecy was often predictive or praying and speaking on behalf of God, calling the people to repent of their sins to avoid the consequences of their disobedience which was God's wrath. In the New Testament, because the scripture was not complete, prophecy was speaking on God's behalf with authority on the Christian experience. Today, prophecy is still delivered through an inspired speaker. Paul understood that these were not the authoritative words of God, but to be tested against the scriptures. Once confirmed, depending upon the message, they were used to either edify, encourage, predict, comfort, rebuke, inspire, correct, or expose wrongdoing. A person with the gift of prophecy, like its Old Testament counterpart, has a keen awareness of current events and the cultural implications of not following God's Word. They are concerned about sin in the church, warn of God's judgment, and exhort the need for repentance.

Benefits. This gift helps the people of the church live holy lives in their own eras and particular cultures. It rebukes, strengthens, and encourages believers. It also helps the church in long-term planning and seeking God for guidance. This gift is important because each church is made up of people, customs, and circumstances that are different from each other. Prophecy helps the church be relevant to their contemporaries and speak to the lifestyle needs of the congregation by helping apply the scriptures to individual circumstances.

Pitfalls. Before speaking about the sins of the church or a contemporary application of truth, a person with the gift of prophecy must be sure that they are hearing from God and not their own inner voice. The temptation of pride can keep this person from being open to discernment and testing to ensure a message is from God. Pride can cause them to have a pharisaical judgment of others while inflating their own importance. Pride makes it hard for a person with this gift to admit when they are wrong, severing the critical need to recheck with God.

Service Opportunities. A person with this gift can serve as part of leadership, and could also participate in a speaking, teaching, or writing ministry.

Further Training. It is important for a person with the gift of prophecy to know the Word of God. This gift can be grown through listening to teachings and sermons and attending conferences that teach the Bible, current events, apologetics, cults and end times. They should have a strong devotional life focused on listening to God. Mentoring with someone who has the gift would help mature this gift.

Passion Rating:		1-5 (1 = low; 5 = high)
Experience Rating:		

NOTES

14. SERVICE

Definition. In Romans 12, Paul writes, "If your gift is serving others, serve them well." In the biblical language, *service* meant "to aid, relieve, help, attend, or to wait on people through menial duties." It is where we get the modern terms deacon, minister, and servant. Service can include almost any work that benefits others. A person with this gift helps with unfinished, often thankless, details as a servant of God and the church. They volunteer to get the job done. This person loves the church and wants to help where they are needed, not minding mundane or labor-intensive tasks.

Benefits. The gift of service frees up pastors and teachers to minister the Word and is an important part of need-based evangelism. The gift of service is an important gift needed to help the church fulfill its responsibilities.

Pitfalls. When needs seem endless and volunteers are few, a person with this gift may overcommit and neglect family and other responsibilities. They must be careful not to become bitter and judge those that don't help. This person may also be tempted by the pride of recognition for their efforts or jealousy if someone outshines them. Service in a ministry is not always like service at a secular corporation. Ministries are budget-challenged, dependent on volunteer staff, and often don't have the best equipment. Because of this, there is usually a shortage of workers and volunteers often don't have the professional skills needed.

Service Opportunities. A person with the gift of service volunteers for routine tasks associated with the church office, classes, programs, and building and grounds. This can include: helping the elderly, organizing or volunteering to help with events, cooking, ushering, visitation, building and ground maintenance, and help with youth and children ministries. In addition to inside the church, there are numerous needs in the community that a person with this gift can address on behalf of the church.

Further Training. A person with this gift can grow through experience, learning perseverance, humility, and determination in accomplishing the tasks that need to be done. This person could benefit from taking classes, reading books, or attending seminars on the topics of leadership, management, project management, and organizational techniques.

Passion Rating:		1-5 (1 = low; 5 = high)
Experience Rating:		

NOTES

_____

_____

_____

_____

_____

_____

_____

_____

_____

15. WISDOM

Definition. In I Corinthians 12, Paul writes, "To one person the Spirit gives the ability to give wise advice." The biblical meaning of the term *wisdom* is "to intelligently apply biblical, spiritual knowledge to a life situation." This insight results in the ability to exercise sound judgment to living a godly life by making scriptural truths relevant and practical in everyday living and decision-making. The gift of wisdom allows a person to know the mind of Christ and his Word as it pertains to specific situations and helps them apply its guiding truth. A person with this gift loves to read, meditate, and commune with God, drawing wisdom from him.

Benefits. God gives this gift to address the many needs in people's lives. From children to the elderly, personal needs are ongoing in matters such as maturity, relationships, emotional health, responsibilities, parenting, and career planning. Wherever people need to increase their understanding, there is a need for wisdom. In all of life, we need to hear the Word of God.

Pitfalls. It is easy for a person with the gift of wisdom to become simplistic in administering God's Word to people's problems. Burnout can cause them to stop listening to people and give standard, cliché answers without tailoring them to the need at hand. This person may be tempted to fake it if they're not sure or rely on human wisdom rather than biblical truth. They need to guard against the temptation of pride that can often come with being wise.

Service Opportunities. The gift of wisdom can be used in counseling, problem-solving, teaching, and leadership, which are all areas of ministry that require wisdom.

Further Training. A person with this gift can grow through the study of the Bible and through education in people-helping skills, such as college classes, conferences, and seminars or specialized certification. If possible, they should find someone else with this gift that will mentor them.

Passion Rating:		1-5 (1 = low; 5 = high)
Experience Rating:		

NOTES

_____

_____

_____

_____

_____

_____

_____

_____

_____

_____

_____

■ PART THREE: EQUIPPING ROLES ■

INSTRUCTIONS FOR COMPLETING PART THREE: Read each of the following five equipping roles descriptions (pages 41-45) in Part Three. Using the scale below, rate your *passion* and *experience* levels for each description. Space is provided for making any personal notes that come to mind as you read through Part Three.

RATING SCALE: 1-5 (1 = low | 2 = somewhat low | 3 = moderate | 4 = somewhat high | 5 = high)

- **Passion.** How motivated are you to take action in this way?
- **Experience.** How much experience do you have with this type of service? How much evidence is there of this role in your life?

1.	PASTOR

Definition. In Ephesians 4:11, Paul writes, "It was He who gave some to be ... pastors." In the original language, the word *pastor* meant *shepherd*. A shepherd watched over, cared for, fed, and attended to the needs of his sheep with an emphasis on the long-term care for the entire flock. In the church, the pastor spiritually cares for and oversees the local flock of Christians. Note: In Ephesians 4:11, Paul combines the role of Pastor with Teacher.

Responsibilities. The modern role of a church pastor has evolved into one that includes: preaching, teaching, leading, administration, counseling and general support/care. With the rise of mega-churches, Senior Pastors require Assistant Pastors and other staff members to help with the care of church members. These assisting roles may be full-time, part-time, or, in many cases, lay pastors. This supporting staff is generally assigned specific duties, such as visitation, discipleship, youth programs, children's programs, administration, Christian education, worship, or missions. Although the Senior Pastor does not care for all aspects of each member of the church, they still serve as overseer and retain the primary responsibilities of leadership, teaching, and preaching.

Training and Qualifications. In I Timothy 3:1-7, Paul provides a list of qualifications for pastors and their staff. Whether the group is small or large, general or a specific care group, certain things must be present. There must be a calling from God, desire to love and care for people and dedication to a spiritual lifestyle. In most denominations/churches, there is a governing body that defers a formal license, commendation, or ordination upon a person after a period of experience and examination. Knowledge of the Bible, theology, and apologetics, as well as skills in pastoral counseling, leadership, conflict resolution, preaching, teaching, and communication, are basic qualifications for the role of leading a church. Depending upon the responsibilities given to them, a lay pastor would need to have a good foundation in the Bible and an outline of a curriculum from their pastor that would include: reading, tapes, taking courses, and attending conferences over time.

Passion Rating:		1-5 (1 = low; 5 = high)
Experience Rating:		

NOTES

_____
_____
_____
_____
_____
_____

Definition. In Ephesians 4:11, Paul writes, "It was He who gave some to be ... evangelists." In the original language, the word *evangelist* meant "a herald, a bearer of good news." In Romans 10:14, he writes, "How, then, can they call on the one they have not believed in? And how can they believe in the one of whom they have not heard? And how can they hear without someone preaching to them? And how can they preach unless they are sent? As it is written, 'How beautiful are the feet of those who bring good news!'" Some take the word evangelist and translate it to mean a gift of evangelism. While I don't deny that there are some of us who seem to be more comfortable leading people to Christ, and I can certainly see this kind of witnessing as an ability given by God, the evangelist is a specific role given by God to share the gospel. Some have translated the word *evangelist* to mean "a traveling missionary," which certainly aligns with Paul's writings. Evangelists often travel from location to location sharing the gospel message. However, with today's technology and the condensed population of mega-cities, a single evangelist can effectively reach multitudes of people without traveling very far.

Responsibilities. The evangelist is responsible to share the gospel. Paul said, "Woe is me if I preach not the gospel." God makes a calling on an evangelist's life, and they are burdened to share the message of salvation with others.

Training and Qualifications. An evangelist certainly needs to know the Bible. Courses in Bible, communication, and speech would help hone necessary skills. The study of current events, and perhaps psychology, might help them understand more of man's current dilemma. The study of church history, missions, prayer, and revival would not only be inspirational but also a model of ministry for them. Like other ministry roles, a good mentor would be beneficial. Experience in an evangelistic organization would also help develop their calling. Finally, a good devotional and prayer life would be the cornerstone of a public ministry.

Passion Rating:		1-5 (1 = low; 5 = high)
Experience Rating:		

NOTES

_____
_____
_____
_____
_____
_____
_____
_____
_____
_____
_____
_____
_____
_____

3. TEACHER

Definition. In Ephesians 4:11, Paul writes, "It was He who gave some to be … teachers." In the original language, the word *teacher* meant "instructor, master, and teacher." The model of teaching in New Testament times was a master/student model. A teacher (master), who had achieved mastery over the subject to be taught, accepted a group of students (disciples). It was not good enough for a teacher to just have knowledge. Students had to learn, which meant the teacher had to have the ability to communicate and instill knowledge into their students. A teacher poured themselves into instructing and guiding their students. We see this model perfectly illustrated in the life of Jesus. We see Jesus teaching his disciples on the road and in the sanctuary and, when teaching, was often addressed as "Master."

Responsibilities. The role of an *equipping* teacher is different from the *gift* of teaching. Paul wrote that God gave these teachers to the Church for the purpose of equipping the believers for service. You can have the gift of teaching and yet not have the role of a teacher that equips the church for service. The emphasis in an equipping role is to pour your teaching into the church to prepare and motivate them for service. As with the other equipping roles, there will be a definite calling on your life to exercise this role. Your calling may be local, regional, or on a larger scale. In any context, it will be obvious to those you teach that you are fulfilling a God-appointed role.

Training and Qualifications. There has been a change in recent history from master/teacher to curriculum-based teaching. Because it's difficult to find teachers with a broad Bible knowledge, Christian education publishers provide a prolific amount of curriculum options, including courses complete with instructor guides and all of the materials needed for teaching each course. Even when these teaching aids are used, teachers need the skills of effective communication and the ability to relate to and meet the needs of those attending their classes or small groups. Individuals in teaching roles should aspire to learn all they can about the Bible and Christian living, as could be accomplished by attending Bible college or taking online courses. Teachers can develop their teaching and communication skills by attending seminars and conferences designed for Christian education teachers.

Passion Rating:		1-5 (1 = low; 5 = high)
Experience Rating:		

NOTES

Definition. In Ephesians 4:11, Paul writes, "It was He who gave some to be ... apostles." In the original language, the word *apostle* means "he that is sent," as in an ambassador or a commissioner of Christ. There were two aspects to the role of Apostle. The first role was foreign church planting. We see Paul going on missionary trips to help start churches. This fits the definition of "one that is sent." The second role is that of an overseer for the churches. We certainly see this in Paul as he wrote letters to the churches he had planted. While not their pastor on a local level, Paul commanded authority and respect as their leader on a regional level.

Responsibilities. As a missionary, an apostle is in charge of planting churches and may have a burden for a particular region. Their life's work revolves around planting churches and helping indigenous pastors continue the work once the church has been established. Apostles see their responsibility as helping many churches succeed in ministry by overseeing the needs of multiple churches on a higher level. The difference between an apostle and pastor is similar to that of a small business owner and an entrepreneur. A pastor is similar to a small business owner with a passion to own their business and is satisfied with running it. An apostle is more like an entrepreneur who feels the need to take the concepts they've learned and apply them to other locations, thus growing the business (e.g. multiple franchises). The modern role of Apostle is displayed in many different ways, such as church consultants that help multiple churches with specific problem areas. God has gifted these people with wisdom and authority to make a difference. Others are called to oversee foreign mission work. Some modern leaders are in charge of multiple church plantings. Perhaps the most popular use of the term is in conjunction with a person serving in a denominational leadership and support role.

Training and Qualifications. This role of Apostle results after years of experience and obvious leading of God. The same guidelines that Paul gives in I Timothy 3:1-7 to those that desire to be an elder also apply to this leader. An apostle needs to have a stellar resume of experience in pastoring, teaching, leadership, encouraging the church and exhibiting faith. This is not the kind of role that someone usually seeks early in life, but as time goes on, life prepares the person for this role.

Passion Rating:		1-5 (1 = low; 5 = high)
Experience Rating:		

NOTES

Definition. In Ephesians 4:11, Paul writes, "It was He who gave some to be ... a prophet." In the original language, the word *prophet* means "inspired speaker." In the Old Testament, a prophet was used to predict God's wrath, prayed on behalf of the people and imparted messages from God. In the New Testament, because the scripture was not complete, the role of Prophet was to speak on God's behalf and with his authority about the Christian experience. According to I Corinthians 14:3, God uses the gift of prophecy on a local level to edify, encourage, and comfort believers. However, just as every pastor is not an apostle, everyone with the gift of prophecy does not have the role of a prophet. Rather than a local church, a prophet has a calling to the larger church. They have the skills and abilities required to use the word of God as a basis for speaking to the church at large about ungodly lifestyles, warning them of judgment, and urging them to repentance. Individuals in the role of Prophet have a burden from God to warn and correct people toward righteousness before it's too late.

Responsibilities. A prophet is in tune with current events and has a burning passion for God's message for their generation. They rebuke, strengthen, and encourage believers. Their ministry also helps the church in long-term planning and seeking God for guidance. In the Old Testament, true prophets were usually recognized as someone with God's anointing and were known by the people as a prophet of God. There were false prophets who spoke lies and predicted events that did not happen, but strict rules required them to be stoned if their words were found to be untrue. Modern prophets must also be tested. Not everyone who calls themselves a prophet today is really God's spokesperson. We need to test their words and ask God for discernment.

Training and Qualifications. John the Baptist, Hosea, Elijah—it's not difficult to spot a prophet. They're consumed with the message that God has given them; warning, rebuking and causing people to repent. They have the skills of an evangelist, passion of a pastor, and a commitment to know God and deliver his message to this generation. This is difficult to train for. There is no Prophet 301 in seminary. God will call out those he wants to use as prophets—those who are prepared for ministry and engaged with teaching and preaching. If God calls you to be a prophet, he will give you a message and an agenda to follow. To prepare and be ready for this calling, study other prophets and mentor with someone that you feel has a prophetic ministry.

Passion Rating:		1-5 (1 = low; 5 = high)
Experience Rating:		

NOTES

_____

_____

_____

_____

_____

_____

_____

_____

_____

_____

_____

PART TWO: SERVICE OPPORTUNITIY DESCRIPTIONS

INSTRUCTIONS: In Part Two (pages 26-40), you rated each spiritual gift based on your passion for and experience with the service opportunities associated with it. Transfer your *passion* and *experience* ratings for each spiritual gift to the scoring chart below.

	Spiritual Gift	Passion Rating	Experience Rating
1	Administration		
2	Discernment		
3	Encouragement		
4	Faith		
5	Giving		
6	Healing		
7	Helping		
8	Teaching		
9	Leadership		
10	Knowledge		
11	Mercy		
12	Miracles		
13	Prophecy		
14	Service		
15	Wisdom		

PART THREE: EQUIPPING ROLES

INSTRUCTIONS: In Part Three (pages 41-45), you rated each equipping role based on your passion for and experience with serving in these roles. Transfer your *passion* and *experience* ratings for each equipping role to the scoring chart below.

	Equipping Role	Passion Rating	Experience Rating
A	Pastor		
B	Evangelist		
C	Teacher		
D	Apostle		
E	Prophet		

QUADRANT CHART: Plot your ratings from the scoring charts on Page 46 on the chart below.

- **Part Two: Service Opportunity Descriptions.** Begin by plotting your scores for "Spiritual Gift #1 – Administration." Locate the intersection of your *passion* and *experience* scores on the chart below and plot it by writing "1" at the corresponding intersection. Use the same procedure for each spiritual gift in the Part Two scoring chart. Plot all fifteen spiritual gifts on the chart below.

- **Part Three: Equipping Roles.** Begin by plotting your scores for "Equipping Role A – Pastor." Locate the intersection of your *passion* and *experience* scores on the chart below and plot it by writing "A" at the corresponding intersection. Use the same procedure for each equipping role in the Part Three scoring chart. Plot all five equipping roles on the chart below.

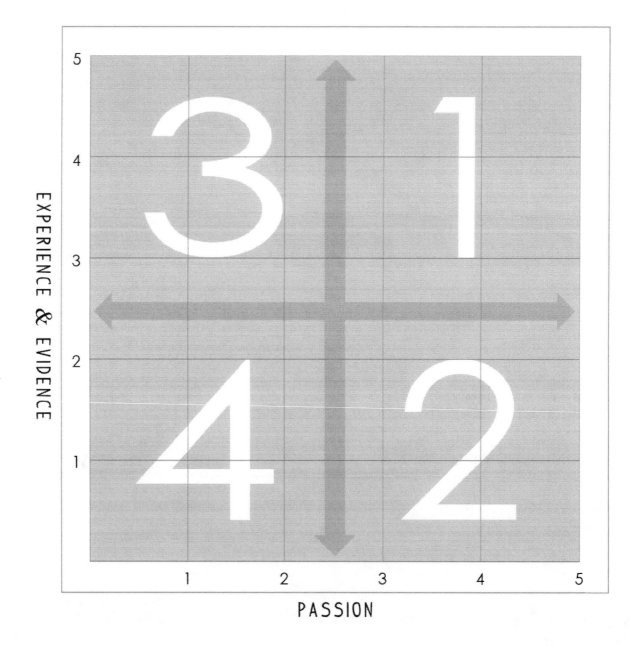

RATING SCALE: 1-5 (1 = low | 2 = somewhat low | 3 = moderate | 4 = somewhat high | 5 = high)

UNDERSTAND YOUR SCORES: Use the descriptions below to interpret the ratings plotted in the quadrant chart on Page 47. *Note: In the rating scale used, 1 = low; 5 = high.*

QUADRANT 1: High Passion & High Experience/Evidence. Scores in this quadrant suggest this is a gift that God has given you. You are passionate about the gift and have experience and evidence in your life that confirm this. Continue to grow in this gift and use it for his glory.

QUADRANT 2: Low Passion & High Experience/Evidence. Scores in this quadrant may indicate that circumstances have called upon you to exhibit this skill or ministry even if you don't have a passion for it. *Example: You don't feel called to help the hungry but may have been recruited to participate in your church's large meal program. Just because you serve in this way doesn't mean that you have the gift of Mercy. It could simply mean that you are obedient to God by helping with a need.*

QUADRANT 3: High Passion and Low Experience/Evidence. Scores in this quadrant are common among the supernatural gifts—healing, faith, and miracles. You may feel genuinely burdened in situations to pray for God's intervention in mighty ways. You pray, believing and trusting that God can and will act. If this is true, then you must rate yourself high on passion. However, though you are passionate in your praying for healing, your experience may not result in supernatural healing and your experience/evidence score is low. This does not mean you should give up. It's just an indicator of your personal experience up to this moment in time. If God moves you deeply to pray for the supernatural, let him take care of the results. It's better to pray, believe, and not see the results you anticipated than to be disobedient and not pray. If God has given you a gift, he will use it according to his will. Be faithful to the passion he has given you.

QUADRANT 4: Low Passion & Low Experience/Evidence. Scores in this quadrant are usually a good indicator that up to this point in time, God has not birthed in you this spiritual gift. God is sovereign and can give any gift at any time to whomever he chooses, so this doesn't mean you'll never be gifted in this area.

■ SPIRITUAL GIFT INVENTORY SUMMARY ■

PART ONE: MINISTRY TASKS (Page 25)

Part One. Refer to the Part One summary section on Page 25. Transfer the *spiritual gifts* you listed in the summary to the chart below.

_____

_____

_____

_____

PART TWO: SERVICE OPPORTUNITY DESCRIPTIONS (Page 47)

Part Two. Refer to the quadrant chart on Page 47. Transfer the spiritual gifts plotted in Quadrant 1 to the chart below.

_____

_____

_____

PART THREE: EQUIPPING ROLES (Page 47)

Part Three. Refer to the quadrant chart on Page 47. Transfer the equipping roles plotted in Quadrant 1 to the chart below.

_____

_____

_____

INSTRUCTIONS: Transfer information in the sections above your **Personal Ministry Profile** in the workbook or e-form.

WIRED for MINISTRY

MINISTRY DRIVES

Your Motivation for Ministry

What really motivates you to minister? What moves you? We call this a personal "drive." Ministry is not just doing what you're good at because of skills, education, and experience. Ministry should also represent the things you're passionate about. How has God wired you when it comes to motivation?

The Ministry Drive Inventory will help you ascertain your personal ministry drives. When completed, the combined scores from Parts One and Two will help you better understand what motivates and drives you when it comes to ministry.

- **Part One.** The first part of the inventory utilizes a definition approach in which you'll read about various drives and rate your passion for each one. Your self-rating will provide an accurate assessment of your passion and inclinations.

- **Part Two.** The second part of the inventory utilizes a forced-choice approach that pairs sets of two different ministry drive behaviors and asks you to choose which one describes you best. Sometimes, your choice will be obvious; other times, you may find some of the paired statements difficult to decide between. The results of forced-choice testing allow deeper examination to consider what your choices indicate about your personal ministry drive.

MINISTRY DRIVE INVENTORY

▨ PART ONE: MINISTRY DRIVE DEFINITIONS ▨

INSTRUCTIONS FOR COMPLETING PART ONE: Part One (pages 52-62) includes eleven ministry drive descriptions. Begin by reading the first ministry drive description ("A - Change Agent") and the characteristics listed below it. Think about the description. How much likeness is there between you and this ministry drive? Use the rating scale below to rate your similarity to this ministry drive description. Use the same procedure to rate each of the ministry drives in Part One. Space is provided for making any personal notes that come to mind as you read through Part One.

RATING SCALE: 1-10 (1 = no likeness | 5 = some likeness | 10 = very accurate)

A. CHANGE AGENT DRIVE		
You have a passion to make things better through change. This motivation is not ego-based. It's born out of a compelling notion that something must be done—there must be a way to change the circumstances.		
Make things more efficient	Change the rules	Make better
Fix	Improve	Advance
Reform	Revise	Shape
Transition	Revolutionize	Develop
Resolve	Transform	Enhance

Rating:		1-10 (1 = no likeness; 10 = very accurate)

NOTES

_____

_____

_____

_____

_____

_____

_____

_____

_____

_____

_____

_____

_____

_____

_____

_____

B. DISCOVERER DRIVE

You respond to the needs of others by exploring new options. Whether the need is great or routine, you have a passion for finding unknown answers to solve problems.

Disclose	Hunt	Examine
Investigate	Discover the truth	Look for a solution
Probe	Reveal	Uncover
Detect	Learn more	Determine
Investigate	Explore	Pursue

Rating:		1-10 (1 = no likeness; 10 = very accurate)

NOTES

_____
_____
_____
_____
_____
_____
_____
_____
_____
_____
_____
_____
_____
_____
_____
_____
_____
_____
_____
_____
_____
_____
_____

C. HELPER DRIVE

You are compelled to help others in almost any situation, in any way possible, and to make a difference. The desire to help is more important to you than the task at hand.

Repair	Restore	Ease
Assist	Relieve	Counsel
Intercede	Serve	Befriend
Encourage	Reach out in compassion	Volunteer
Comfort	Accommodate	Support

Rating:		1-10 (1 = no likeness; 10 = very accurate)

NOTES

_____
_____
_____
_____
_____
_____
_____
_____
_____
_____
_____
_____
_____
_____
_____
_____
_____
_____
_____
_____
_____
_____
_____
_____

D. PROPHET DRIVE

You are motivated to speak with a passion for truth and justice by pointing out injustice and evil in a way that encourages and comforts others.

Warn	Forecast	Provide foresight
Inspect	Anticipate	Foresee
Act as a watchdog	Be a lookout	Monitor
Sound the alarm	Give caution	Motivate
Encourage	Speak the truth	Predict

Rating:	1-10 (1 = no likeness; 10 = very accurate)

NOTES

E. CREATIVE DRIVE

You have a burning desire to express yourself through art, writing, music, speaking, acting, or another artistic expression. You are compelled to create beauty and consider it your calling.

Produce	Bring into being	Establish
Innovate	Create ideas	Imagine
Construct	Invent	Conceive
Institute	Originate	Organize
Arrange	Design	Portray

Rating:		1-10 (1 = no likeness; 10 = very accurate)

NOTES

_____
_____
_____
_____
_____
_____
_____
_____
_____
_____
_____
_____
_____
_____
_____
_____
_____
_____
_____
_____
_____
_____
_____
_____

F. PROTECTOR DRIVE

You are motivated to safeguard causes that they care deeply about. You have a passion to defend, warn, and prevent negative consequences from happening to others.

Shelter	Shield	Screen
Preserve	Save	Secure
Prevent	Take precautions	Assure
Guard	Defend	Safeguard
Deliver	Conserve	Cover

Rating:	1-10 (1 = no likeness; 10 = very accurate)

NOTES

_____
_____
_____
_____
_____
_____
_____
_____
_____
_____
_____
_____
_____
_____
_____
_____
_____
_____
_____
_____
_____
_____
_____
_____

G. PROVIDER DRIVE

You are passionate about supplying what is needed to nurture and sustain others. Even if you don't personally have the resources needed, you're compelled to find those that do.

Giver	Donor	Underwrite
Support	Provide	Contribute
Replenish	Nurture	Accommodate
Grant	Care for	Prepare
Supply	Subsidize	Equip

Rating:		1-10 (1 = no likeness; 10 = very accurate)

NOTES

_____
_____
_____
_____
_____
_____
_____
_____
_____
_____
_____
_____
_____
_____
_____
_____
_____
_____
_____
_____
_____
_____
_____
_____

H. PROMOTER DRIVE

You are motivated to act and get others involved. When you see a cause, you want to champion it. Words and phrases that might better express your tendency to relate to a cause with this ministry drive are:

Crusade	Network	Tell everyone
Champion	Organize	Upgrade
Boost	Publicize	Uphold
Advance	Advocate	Urge
Elevate	Foster	Create public acceptance

Rating:		1-10 (1 = no likeness; 10 = very accurate)

NOTES

_____
_____
_____
_____
_____
_____
_____
_____
_____
_____
_____
_____
_____
_____
_____
_____
_____
_____
_____
_____
_____
_____
_____
_____
_____

I. PEACEMAKER DRIVE

You are compelled to find fair and righteous solutions that are good for all parties involved. You're able to remain impartial when dealing with opposing opinions and disagreements and like to focus on win-win solutions.

Arbitrate	Referee	Judge
Mediate	Help people get along	Work toward the better good
Synthesize	Reconcile	Bring understanding
Appease	Intervene	Merge
Negotiate	Compromise	Assimilate

Rating:		1-10 (1 = no likeness; 10 = very accurate)

NOTES

_____
_____
_____
_____
_____
_____
_____
_____
_____
_____
_____
_____
_____
_____
_____
_____
_____
_____
_____
_____
_____
_____
_____

J. LEADER DRIVE

You are motivated to look for areas that need direction and enjoy using your skills to make things happen. You're a strategic thinker, able to see the big picture, motivate people, bring cohesiveness, and help causes reach their goals.

Guide	Conduct	Influence
Head	Administrate	Create vision
Lead the way	Direct	Consult
Oversee	Oversee	Oversee
Supervise	Pilot	Manage

Rating:	1-10 (1 = no likeness; 10 = very accurate)

NOTES

K. ORGANIZER DRIVE

You are passionate about shaping details into a functioning order, plan, or system to get things done. You have an ability to create and implement structures that will effectively administrate the details needed to bring a solution to completion.

Establish	Classify	Unscramble
Provide structure	Mobilize	Administrate
Institute	Layout in sequence	Create order
Sort	Orchestrate	Map and align
Draw up	Arrange	Prioritize

Rating:	1-10 (1 = no likeness; 10 = very accurate)

NOTES

▦ PART ONE: SCORING ▦

PART ONE SCORING INSTRUCTIONS: Read through Part One and transfer your rating for each ministry drive to the chart below.

	MINISTRY DRIVE	RATING
A	Change Agent	
B	Discoverer	
C	Helper	
D	Prophet	
E	Creative	
F	Protector	
G	Provider	
H	Promoter	
I	Peacemaker	
J	Leader	
K	Organizer	

▦ PART ONE: SUMMARY ▦

PART ONE SUMMARY: Based on your ratings in the scoring chart above, determine your top four and lowest two ministry drives and list them below.

TOP FOUR MINISTRY DRIVES

1 _____

2 _____

3 _____

4 _____

LOWEST TWO MINISTRY DRIVES

1 _____

2 _____

▓ PART TWO: MINISTRY DRIVE BEHAVIORS ▓

INSTRUCTIONS FOR COMPLETING PART TWO: Pairs of phrases are organized into five sections in Part Two (pages 64-68). Each section includes a beginning phrase and a list of paired ending phrases. Begin in Section 1 by reading the beginning phrase ("When a problem moves me deeply, I...") followed by the first pair of ending phrases in the list below it.

Think about each sentence created by the two ending phrases. Check the phrase that completes the sentence in a way that describes you best. Even if neither phrase or both phrases describe you, check the phrase that describes you best. Check only one ending phrase in each pair. Use the same procedure to respond to each of the ministry drive sentences in this inventory. Space is provided for making any personal notes that come to mind as you read through Part Two.

SECTION 1: When a problem moves me deeply, I ...

	ENDING PHRASE			ENDING PHRASE	
○	want to move toward making modifications.	A	○	want to repair what is broken.	A
○	want to relieve the immediate situation.	C	○	unearth what the problem is.	B
○	search for a better way to handle the situation.	B	○	befriend those who are hurting.	C
○	warn others about the problem.	D	○	volunteer to help supervise.	J
○	negotiate the best solution.	I	○	communicate artistically what is wrong.	E
○	create music or art to express the problem.	E	○	be a champion for the cause.	H
○	contribute to those helping the situation.	G	○	make things change for the better.	A
○	help in areas that need leadership.	J	○	create a plan to make a difference.	K
○	uncover the reason behind the problem.	B	○	offer to help arbitrate a win/win solution.	I
○	marshal a group to help bring a solution.	K	○	be on the lookout in case it happens again.	D
○	shelter the victims.	F	○	help underwrite the cost to take care of it.	G
○	get people involved in a solution.	H	○	defend people from the problem.	F

NOTES

_____

_____

_____

_____

_____

_____

_____

_____

_____

_____

_____

SECTION 2: I get deep satisfaction from ...

ENDING PHRASE

○	solving a complex problem.	B
○	making something new.	E

○	correcting a bad situation.	A
○	being able to predict a bad situation in time.	D

○	protecting the innocent.	F
○	bringing peace to a situation.	I

○	contributing somehow to a worthy cause.	G
○	volunteering to help someone.	C

○	looking for a solution.	B
○	inspiring change through art.	E

○	helping prevent evil.	D
○	helping a team reach its goal.	J

○	making things better.	A
○	making people aware of a great opportunity.	H

ENDING PHRASE

○	defending those who can't defend themselves.	F
○	negotiating a solution.	I

○	comforting someone who is down.	C
○	warning people before it's too late.	D

○	mobilizing people to make a difference.	K
○	defending those that need it.	F

○	networking to help solve a problem.	H
○	helping donate to a serious need.	G

○	creating something beautiful.	E
○	overseeing a project.	J

○	bringing order out of a chaotic situation.	K
○	helping by doing what is required of me.	C

NOTES

73

SECTION 3: To solve a problem I care about, I would ...

ENDING PHRASE		
○	creatively communicate about the problem.	E
○	volunteer to help any way I can.	C
○	intercede on behalf of the problem.	I
○	make the situation better.	A
○	warn people and speak against the problem.	D
○	give to those solving the problem.	G
○	try to prevent it from happening again.	F
○	detect the underlying causes.	B
○	serve those who are hurting any way I can.	C
○	be an advocate on their behalf.	H
○	furnish needed resources.	G
○	institute a solution.	K
○	create literature or videos about the problem.	E
○	help create a vision for the solution.	J

ENDING PHRASE		
○	administrate a plan of action.	K
○	bring awareness to the situation.	H
○	bring people together to solve the problem.	I
○	find a better way to solve the problem.	B
○	organize an incredible program.	K
○	bring relief to those hurting.	C
○	foresee the situation and alert people.	D
○	make the situation more stable.	F
○	supply what I could to make a difference.	G
○	lead a crusade against the problem.	A
○	supervise where needed most.	J
○	revise what is being done wrong.	A

NOTES

SECTION 4: If I could, I would like a career that includes …

ENDING PHRASE		ENDING PHRASE	
○ championing a cause.	H	○ using my imagination.	E
○ creating something beautiful.	E	○ preserving something from being destroyed.	F
○ warning people about evil.	D	○ unlocking mysteries.	B
○ creating plans of action.	K	○ championing an idea.	H
○ negotiating.	I	○ doing something to help people.	C
○ being beneficial to the community.	C	○ improving on existing systems.	A
○ saving people from a terrible situation.	F	○ being a watchdog against evil.	D
○ upper management, supervising a group.	J	○ discovering something new.	B
○ giving back to those who need help.	G	○ guiding a coalition toward a high goal.	J
○ warning people about a serious problem.	D	○ arranging details to produce results.	K
○ inventing something useful.	E	○ saving the world from a problem.	F
○ organizing solutions.	K	○ sharing predictions of coming problems.	D
○ arranging events to help promote a cause.	H	○ helping people work together.	I
○ arbitrating peace.	I	○ giving back to those in need.	G
○ transforming situations into better ones.	A	○ bringing change through intercession.	I
○ using my creativity.	E	○ helping those in need.	C
○ allowing me to discover something important.	B	○ organizing events.	H
○ consulting management on leadership.	J	○ coaching a project team.	J
○ helping people.	C	○ helping give to those in need.	G
○ warning people about evil.	D	○ expressing myself artistically.	E
○ allowing me to improve a bad situation.	A	○ finding new solutions to problems.	B
○ preserving what is right.	F	○ mentoring people on leadership.	J
○ changing things for the better.	A	○ helping people get along.	I
○ contributing to needy causes.	G	○ establishing productive systems.	K
○ be a watchdog for an important cause.	D		
○ defend the innocent.	F		

NOTES

75

ENDING PHRASE			ENDING PHRASE	
○ reformer.	A	○ preserver.	F
○ organizer.	K	○ Creative.	E
○ discoverer.	B	○ artist.	E
○ helper.	C	○ peacemaker.	I
○ mediator.	I	○ giver.	G
○ change agent.	A	○ fixer.	A
○ investigator.	B	○ project manager.	J
○ protector.	F	○ sponsor.	H
○ helper.	C	○ deliverer.	F
○ coach.	J	○ reformer.	A
○ administrator.	K	○ team leader.	J
○ explorer.	B	○ change agent.	A
○ artist.	E	○ fundraiser.	G
○ promoter.	H	○ comforter.	C
○ futurist.	D	○ champion.	H
○ negotiator.	I	○ watchdog.	D
○ creative.	E	○ leader.	J
○ mobilizer.	K	○ administrator.	K
○ researcher.	B	○ helper.	C
○ provider.	G	○ supporter.	G
○ supervisor.	J	○ backer.	H
○ prophet.	D	○ protector.	F
○ mediator.	I	○ referee.	I
○ organizer.	K	○ discoverer.	B
○ advocate.	H		
○ donor.	G		

NOTES

_____

_____

_____

_____

_____

PART TWO SCORING INSTRUCTIONS: Each ending phrase in Part Two has a designated *ministry drive* letter (A, B, C, etc.) located next to it in the right-hand column. Begin by going back through each section in Part Two (pages 40-43). Count the number of times you checked phrases that are designated with the letter "*A*" and record it in the chart below on the line next to "*A: Change Agent.*"

EXAMPLE: If you checked, "*...want to move toward making modifications,*" in the first pair, record it as shown below.

	MINISTRY DRIVE		TOTAL
A	Change Agent	\	

Continue through Part Two, recording the number of times you checked phrases for the remaining ministry drives listed below (B-K). Only record the ending phrases you checked. Use the same procedure for each ministry drive until all checked phrases have been recorded in the chart below. Add the numbers together horizontally for each ministry drive and write the sum in the *Total* column.

	MINISTRY DRIVE	NUMBER OF TIMES EACH LETTER WAS CHECKED	TOTAL
A	Change Agent		
B	Discoverer		
C	Helper		
D	Prophet		
E	Creative		
F	Protector		
G	Provider		
H	Promoter		
I	Peacemaker		
J	Leader		
K	Organizer		

■ PART TWO: INTERPRETING RESULTS ■

UNDERSTANDING YOUR SCORE: The most points you can have for each ministry drive is sixteen. These scores represent the way you react to various causes. Higher scores indicate a likelihood that you are motivated to react to a cause in this way and have a passion for being involved using this ministry drive. Mid-range and lower scores may reflect a moderate interest or may be the result of interest in similar ministry drives which splits the scores between more dominant drives.

16-13: Dominant Ministry Drive. You have a passion for responding to causes in this way. If you're not already involved in helping causes in this way, do some research in this ministry drive, seek others who operate through this drive, and explore how you might get involved helping people through it.

12-9: Strong Ministry Drive. You have a strong desire to be involved helping a cause in this way. Your score could also reflect an interest in two or three similar drives, thus splitting the score rather than having one ministry drive more dominant than the others. Please review your answers or go to the *Wired for Ministry* workbook and review the Ministry Drive Inventory for more understanding. We encourage you to pursue the drives that you feel strongly about.

8-below: Moderate to Low Ministry Drive. Depending on your score, you may have some interest in helping causes in this way. A lower score may also reflect an interest in two or three similar drives, thus splitting the score rather than having one ministry drive more dominant than the others. If this is the case, please continue to pursue your interest in that drive and work toward perfecting skills in that area.

▓ MINISTRY DRIVE INVENTORY SUMMARY ▓

INSTRUCTIONS: Based on the information you recorded in the Part One summary on Page 63 and the totals from the scoring chart on Page 69, list your top four ministry drives below. Transfer this summary information to your **Personal Ministry Profile in** the workbook or e-form.

TOP FOUR MINISTRY DRIVES

1 _____

2 _____

3 _____

4 _____

MINISTRY PREFERENCES

Your Passion for Ministry

skills   education   experience   spiritual gifts   ministry drives   **MINISTRY PREFERENCES**

W hat areas of service interest you? What types of ministry tasks do you enjoy doing? In this section, you'll determine the types of ministries that appeal to you. The two-part Ministry Preference Inventory considers your interest in and passion for different types of ministries. The emphasis is on your *personal interest* in specific ministries and how you *enjoy* using your passion, abilities, spiritual gifts, and experience to serve God.

- **Part One.** In Part One, you'll review a detailed list of specific service tasks associated with various church or local para-church ministries. This list is not meant to be comprehensive. There are many other tasks associated with various ministries, however, this list provides you with a wide variety of individual service tasks to help you think about how you might be interested in serving. *For example, you may not be interested in helping with the middle school youth group but might enjoy transporting young people to events or keeping church buses in good working order.*

- **Part Two.** Part Two utilizes a definition-based approach and organizes various types of ministries into broad categories. You'll read each of the twenty ministry type definitions and rate the category according to your *interest* and *passion* level. Each ministry definition includes a list of roles commonly associated with that ministry. Reviewing ministry type roles will assist you in gauging your preference for each ministry type as a whole.

MINISTRY PREFERENCE INVENTORY

■ PART ONE: SERVICE TASKS ■

INSTRUCTIONS FOR COMPLETING PART ONE: Part One (pages 73-74) includes a list of one hundred seventy service tasks that correlate to twenty different types of ministry. Using the rating scale below, rate each service task according to how much it *interests* and *appeals* to you. For each task listed, consider how much you would *enjoy* participating in it and to what extent you consider it to be one of your preferred areas of service. Note: This rating scale does not include "3." Use only 1, 2, 4 or 5. Space is provided for making any personal notes that come to mind as you read through Part One.

RATING SCALE: 1-5 (1 = little interest | 2 = some interest | *3* = do not use | 4 = moderate interest | 5 = high interest)

RATE	SERVICE TASK	TYPE	RATE	SERVICE TASK	TYPE
	Work on the church strategic plan	7		Join others praying about church issues	7
	Take meals to shut-ins	4		Research materials for Christian education	9
	Lead youth small group	1		Assist in mailings	6
	Serve on missions team	18		Assist with the sound system	17
	Teach evangelism course	3		Pray with an individual about personal issues	10
	Help with food for meetings & events	16		Lead evangelistic Bible study	3
	Assist in disaster clean-up	5		Pray with others for a church revival	19
	Organize sports ministry	20		Work with construction ministry	5
	Setup computer network	15		Keep in contact with missionaries	18
	Direct a drama	12		Help a person organize & finish a task	10
	Preach a sermon	19		Lead Bible study	9
	Assist in church landscaping	8		Transport young people	1
	Assist in nursery	2		Help serve food at church functions	16
	Help to equip teachers	9		Visit with people recuperating at home	4
	Lead adult Sunday school	14		Help with wardrobe & makeup for drama	12
	Manage an office	6		Update church on mission news	18
	Provide meals for the suffering	5		Help with accounting	6
	Schedule rehearsals	11		Edit videos	17
	Make signs, posters & brochures	13		Serve with recreational ministry	20
	Work with fiscal management	7		Facilitate a meeting	7
	Transport the elderly	4		Sing with praise team	11
	Create databases	15		Work in church-based job ministry	5
	Plan youth activities	1		Participate in prayer ministry	19
	Write skits/dramas	12		Teach parenting skills	14
	Participate in church clean-up days	8		Make home visits to those new at church	4
	Teach children's Sunday school	2		Coach/mentor life skills	10
	Lead support group	10		Share my personal testimony	3
	Lead single adult ministry	14		Take minutes at meetings	6
	Comfort those who are sick	4		Oversee day-to-day functioning of the church	19
	Help with large banquet	16		Help church use its resources efficiently	7
	Help people learn the Bible	9		Volunteer to help with sports program	20
	Design web and social media	13		Organize men's breakfast	14
	Lead children in games	2		Mentor a young person	1
	Participate in camping ministry	20		Paint a mural	13
	Assist with computer needs	15		Assist with mission/vision	7
	Help make phone calls for meetings	6		Volunteer with Vacation Bible School	2
	Work with addictions ministry	5		Work with local mission projects	18
	Assist with youth retreat	1		Organize marriage seminars	14

RATE	SERVICE TASK	TYPE	RATE	SERVICE TASK	TYPE
	Distribute gospel literature	3		Storyboard videos	17
	Repair and maintain vehicles	8		Participate on the building committee	8
	Organize short-term missions trip	18		Lead games on youth night	1
	Play instrument in praise band	11		Work in food pantry	16
	Teach a Bible study	19		Coordinate music distribution	11
	Beautify the sanctuary	13		Work on stage sets	12
	Assist in cultural events at church	20		Market church through social media	15
	Teach toddler Sunday school	2		Operate audio/visual during church service	17
	Help clean church	8		Work with homeless shelter	5
	Consult on sound system	17		Teach crafts & games to children	2
	Help referee sports events	20		Get Christmas gifts for missionaries	18
	Answer phones in office	6		Help decorate for events	16
	Lead singing	11		Create and/or maintain website	15
	Work with city-wide evangelistic outreach	3		Create and/or find music arrangements	11
	Express myself through photography	13		Give gospel presentation to group	3
	Recruit teachers	9		Host adult small group fellowships	14
	Perform in dramas	12		Find age/group-specific church curriculum	9
	Work with food/clothing ministry	5		Visit, comfort & pray with people at home	19
	Operate camera for video production	17		Decorate church for holidays	13
	Create recreational outreach events	20		Give relief to those caring for the dying	4
	Be an accountability partner	10		Sponsor someone with addiction	10
	Help paint church	8		Work as stagehand for drama	12
	Assist with Information Technology	15		Assist with parking needs	8
	Help children's ministry administration	2		Prepare desserts for meals	16
	Organize Sunday school	9		Assist with printing	6
	Serve on church governing board	7		Organize men's or women's group	14
	Work with youth/children music	11		Serve in church leadership	19
	Visit elderly at home or in nursing homes	4		Teach seminars on emotional issues	10
	Serve in kitchen clean-up	16		Set up audio/visual presentations	17
	Create graphics and illustrations	13		Organize missions conference/ministry fair	18
	Assist with youth missions trip	1		Invite people to gospel presentation	3
	Perform dramatic storytelling	12		Set up computer learning center	15

■ PART ONE: SCORING ■

PART ONE SCORING INSTRUCTIONS: Part One (pages 73-74) includes seven service tasks for each ministry type listed below. Begin by scanning down through the right-hand column next to each service task to locate the seven tasks designated as type "1." Transfer your rating for each of those service tasks to the chart below next to "1 – Youth" in the space provided.

EXAMPLE: If you rated ministry tasks designated as ministry type "1" (Youth) as "1's" and "2's," record them as follows:

	MINISTRY TYPE								TOTAL
1	Youth	1	1	2	1	2	1	1	9

Continue through Part One, recording your ratings for each of the other ministry types (2-20) in the scoring chart below. Add the numbers together horizontally for each ministry type and write the sum in the Total column.

	MINISTRY TASK RATINGS FOR EACH MINISTRY TYPE								
	MINISTRY TYPE	1	2	3	4	5	6	7	TOTAL
1	Youth								
2	Children								
3	Evangelism								
4	Visitation								
5	Mercy								
6	Office Administration								
7	Leadership								
8	Maintenance								
9	Christian Education								
10	Counseling/Mentoring								
11	Music								
12	Drama/Speech								
13	Visual Arts								
14	Adult								
15	Computer Technology								
16	Food Services								
17	Media								
18	Missions								
19	Pastoral Duties								
20	Leisure/Recreation								

▓ PART ONE: INTERPRETING RESULTS ▓

UNDERSTANDING YOUR SCORE: The most points you can have for each ministry type is thirty-five points—seven scores for each ministry type with the maximum of five points each. The Total column represents your collective preference regarding each type of ministry. The higher the rating, the more passion you have for this type of serving. There are many opportunities to serve professionally or as a lay person in each ministry type. A good way to validate your score is to ask a close friend or relative for feedback. If others rate you differently, pray about it and find someone who is already doing it well to learn more. Mid-range and lower scores may reflect a moderate interest or may be the result of interest in similar ministry types which splits the scores between what would otherwise appear as dominant preferences.

35-30: Dominant Ministry Preference. You have a passion for serving in this type of ministry. If you're not already involved in helping causes in this type of ministry, do some research in this ministry drive, seek others who operate through this drive and explore how you might get involved.

29-25: Strong Ministry Preference. You have a strong desire to serve in this type of ministry. Your score could also reflect interests in two or three similar ministries, thus splitting the score rather than having one ministry preference more dominant than the others.

24-20: Moderate Ministry Preference. You have some interest in serving in this type of ministry, but it's not a strong preference. Your score could also reflect interests in two or three similar drives, thus splitting the score rather than having one ministry drive more dominant than the others.

19-below: Low Ministry Preference. You have little passion for serving in this type of ministry at this time.

▓ PART ONE: SUMMARY ▓

INSTRUCTIONS: Review your Part One scores on Page 75. Based on the highest totals, determine your top three ministry preferences and list them below. Transfer this summary information to your **Personal Ministry Profile in** the workbook or e-form.

TOP 3 MINISTRY PREFERENCES

1 _____
2 _____
3 _____

▓ PART TWO: MINISTRY TYPES ▓

INSTRUCTIONS FOR COMPLETING PART TWO: Part Two (pages 77-96) includes twenty ministry type descriptions. Begin by reading the first ministry type— "Youth Ministry"—including the areas of ministry associated with this type of ministry. Think about the description and highlight or underline parts of the description that really interest you. Consider the ministry type as a whole, and rate your interest using the rating scale below. Use the same procedure to rate each of the ministry types in Part Two. Space is provided for making any personal notes that come to mind as you read through Part One.

RATING SCALE: 1-5 (1 = not interested | 3 = somewhat interested | 5 = very interested)

1. YOUTH MINISTRY

You believe that to be known, important, and loved can change someone's outlook on life. You have a passion to give young people a place to go and learn to worship God, his nature, his plans for them and their future. You know the importance of leaders and role models in the lives of young people and are willing to help in any way that you can. You relate well to teenagers and have their respect. You understand adolescence—the fears, temptations, and struggles— and are willing to be patient, loving, and pray for them. You enjoy helping teens integrate into the larger, intergenerational community of the church and find ways to help them participate as co-creators and conspirators in the divine work of the church.

Areas of Ministry:
Teach junior high, high school, or college age Sunday school; be a youth director or youth counselor; teach at a Christian school; be a camp counselor; chaperone during youth events; host youth activities; prayer supporter; church youth task committee member; retreat volunteer; games coordinator; volunteer on youth nights; drive you to events; life skills mentor; tutor; provide support to parents/teens in conflict; drug counselor; big brother/sister; adolescent/family counselor; and college/career guidance counselor.

Rating:		**1-5** (1 = not interested; 5 = very interested)

NOTES

_____

_____

_____

_____

_____

_____

_____

_____

_____

_____

_____

2. CHILDREN'S MINISTRY

You believe that children are our future and that they need a solid spiritual foundation. You love to be with children and help them experience the love of Jesus. Parents will likely attend a church where their children want to go, so you're dedicated to making sure their children are loved and discipled. You have patience, a good sense of humor, and children like to be around you. You understand childhood developmental stages and can help children grow. Life happens in relationships, so you're dedicated to mentoring and coaching children to create and maintain Christ-centered relationships that will last a lifetime. You know how difficult the parenting process is and are dedicated to supporting parents by loving their children unconditionally.

Areas of Ministry:

Teach Sunday school; supervise in the Christian education program; nursery attendant; Christian pre-school or elementary school teacher; song leader; games director; VBS volunteer; Bible Club worker; MOPS volunteer; daycare specialist; special education worker; pediatric medicine; child psychologist; family counselor; and respite care.

Rating:		**1-5** (1 = not interested; 5 = very interested)

NOTES

3. EVANGELISM MINISTRY

You believe that effective evangelism is God's will for the church and are burdened for the lost. You proactively share the gospel and willing share your testimony and the plan of salvation. Your house is a place where you participate in friendship evangelism through lifestyle and relationships. You believe in reaching the community by helping them through needs-based evangelism, fusing social outreach with the gospel message. At work, you share the love of Christ through your life example and try to be a witness in the way you live so not to bring reproach against Christ. You feel the church should reach out to the neighborhood and are willing to help in any way that you can.

Areas of Ministry:

Participate on the church evangelism team; serve on the mission committee; set up literature distribution; teach evangelism; church greeter; visitor engagement; conduct door-to-door surveys and distribute literature; evangelistic preaching; work on community project teams; benchmark evangelistic programs and find ways to integrate new ideas; meet needs and give your testimony; participate in prayer meetings for revival; partner with other churches on evangelistic campaigns to capitalize on the power of cooperation; and assist with and support evangelistic outreach efforts.

Rating:		**1-5** (1 = not interested; 5 = very interested)

NOTES

4. VISITATION MINISTRY

You believe that whether visiting people in their homes or in the hospital, the simple act of connecting with others is filled with powerful possibilities. Your heart goes out to the sick and elderly and seek to relate to them with the compassion and love of Jesus. You enjoy listening to people's personal stories and communicating the current events of your church. You find great joy in taking meals, cleaning houses, or doing yard work for those that can't. You gladly take people shopping, to doctor appointments, hairdressers/barbers, and out for meals. You count it a privilege to pray for those that are dying and bring comfort in any way that you can. You've studied the development stages of aging, empathize with their situation, and want to help them feel valued and maintain a level of dignity.

Areas of Ministry:
Take meals; read to an individual or a group; visit regularly in homes and care facilities; prayer; advocate for the needs of the sick and elderly in your church; set up a visitation team; organize work crews to help with home repairs; visit those that are sick from your congregation and pray for them; work at a retirement or nursing home; set up an emergency fund for those on a fixed income; bring the elderly to children's events; set up luncheons and events for the elderly; and help shut-ins be useful members of the church and community by including them in tasks they can do.

Rating:		**1-5** (1 = not interested; 5 = very interested)

NOTES

_____
_____
_____
_____
_____
_____
_____
_____
_____
_____
_____
_____
_____
_____
_____
_____
_____
_____
_____
_____

5. COMMUNITY MINISTRY

You believe that impacting the community by helping the needy follows the model of Christ and is a priority of the church. You are moved when you hear about the spiritual, material, physical, financial, emotional, intellectual, or social needs of others. You are action-oriented and want to help in any way that you can. You know about community development and church outreach programs and volunteer on your own or with your church to help those in need. You enjoy serving in a way that helps people see, sense and experience that you care about them and that God loves them. You are passionate about leveraging the church's time, energy and resources back out into the community so people will see, sense, and experience God's love through the care they receive.

Areas of Ministry:

Volunteer for community programs; organize a food pantry, clothes drive, or urban mission trip; help those in your church with needs; update your church with community development opportunities; start a mentoring program at your church; advocate for child care, foster care and adoption; involve your church in blood drives; mentor teenage mothers; help with job readiness, retention and advancement training; provide summer jobs or internships; get involved in community politics to bring about change; be a Big Brother/Sister; work on affordable housing projects; teach parenting skills; be a home visitor; volunteer your medical expertise; and be an advocate for health issues.

Rating:		**1-5** (1 = not interested; 5 = very interested)

NOTES

_____

_____

_____

_____

_____

_____

_____

_____

_____

_____

_____

_____

_____

_____

_____

_____

_____

_____

_____

_____

_____

6. OFFICE ADMINISTRATION MINISTRY

You understand the administrative effort it takes for a church or ministry to function, so you help in any way that you can. You believe that church administration is a spiritual service to the Body of Christ and involves the wise stewardship of God's resources for the accomplishment of ministry. You assist with office duties and volunteer to use your clerical, accounting, marketing, office management, organizational or executive skills when needed. You help with the acquisition of office equipment, such as computers, printers, and office furniture to ensure office administration runs smoothly.

Areas of Ministry:

Volunteer to help with mailings, answer phones, or help with bulletins; help with accounting; assist with office space planning and equipment purchase, set-up or maintenance; assist in printing needs; manage the information on bulletin boards; assist with the website; train administrative staff in your field of expertise; assist in the marketing and advertising needs of the church; support church committees by setting up meetings; and help send out church announcements.

Rating:		**1-5** (1 = not interested; 5 = very interested)

NOTES

7. LEADERSHIP MINISTRY

You believe that one of the most important things church members and visitors are looking for is effective and engaging leadership in a church. You like things to be done effectively and use your managerial experience to help the church and its ministries run smoothly. You're a servant leader, willing to sit on committees and help any way that you can. You strive to live according to 1 Timothy 3 and pray regularly for your pastor and church board, committees, and programs. You stand ready to assist with leadership issues when needed and consider leadership positions, such as deacon/deaconess, to be a sacred duty. You keep up with the latest in church leadership materials, attend training, when possible, and disseminate what you learn to the rest of the church leadership team.

Areas of Ministry:

Serve as an elder or deacon/deaconess; participate on or lead church/para-church committees; encourage and motive members, staff and visitors; attend or lead prayer meetings; volunteer to rally support for events; meet regularly with the pastor to pray for the church and its committees/programs; assist in leadership using your expertise; serve on the board of local ministry; participate in strategic planning and vision casting; assist with leadership development by mentoring others; help communicate vision for the church; and assist in fund raising for major church or para-church projects.

Rating:		**1-5** (1 = not interested; 5 = very interested)

NOTES

_____
_____
_____
_____
_____
_____
_____
_____
_____
_____
_____
_____
_____
_____
_____
_____
_____
_____
_____
_____

8. MAINTENANCE MINISTRY (Buildings, Grounds & Vehicles)

You believe the appearance and functionality of the church or local ministry is a testimony to the neighborhood and community. You support ministries through the care and maintenance of church equipment, buildings, and vehicles to ensure facilities operate smoothly, safely, and with excellence. You use your specialized expertise to accomplish all that you can within the fiscal limits of the church or ministry.

Areas of Ministry:

Help keep vehicles running; set up maintenance schedules; post maintenance needs on the church events calendar to recruit volunteers; help set up and/or tear down chairs, tables and equipment; volunteer to drive church vehicles; serve on a committee to assure safety of building, grounds, vehicles and their appropriate use; conduct safety training; participate on or oversee the janitorial crew; volunteer for painting, carpentry, repairing and landscaping duties; use your personal knowledge and network to negotiate quality and fair-priced goods and services; and donate toward needed equipment.

Rating:	1-5 (1 = not interested; 5 = very interested)

NOTES

_____
_____
_____
_____
_____
_____
_____
_____
_____
_____
_____
_____
_____
_____
_____
_____
_____
_____
_____
_____

9. CHRISTIAN EDUCATION MINISTRY

You believe that the church body should know the Word and how to apply it to their lives. You like to teach, have a passion for specific Christian topics and like to share your knowledge with others. You're a good communicator, able to engage the audience, and have an excellent working knowledge of the subjects you teach. You believe that biblical depth equips people for successful Christina living and you enjoy leading discussions that prompt people to dig deeper to increase their understanding of God. You believe that the church should be a resource to its people and strive to provide the best educational resources possible.

Areas of Ministry:

Set up a church library/resource center; teach Sunday school, adult home Bible studies, youth groups, or senior citizen groups; serve as a Sunday School superintendent; represent the church by teaching at church seminars; mentor others to become students and deepen their knowledge of the Word; provide teacher training; advocate for, acquire, and maintain optimal classroom equipment; strive to get others in the community to attend teaching sessions in the church; arrange for guest speakers to teach at your church on relevant topics; and update your church with educational opportunities.

Rating:		**1-5** (1 = not interested; 5 = very interested)

NOTES

10. COUNSELING/MENTORING MINISTRY

You have empathy for those that are hurting emotionally and socially and are passionate about helping people overcome their problems, find meaning and joy in life and become healthy and well-adjusted individuals. You know that emotional, psychological, and social suffering is complex but believe that people can make changes and return to joy if they are shown how to go about it. You're not overly simplistic in seeking solutions, believe in the power of mentoring and contribute in any way that you can. You advocate for those you're seeking to help and recruit volunteers to assist in providing technical, emotional or spiritual help. You organize, promote, and participate in support groups that provide comfort and assistance to those that are hurting.

Areas of Ministry:

Set up or participate in a counseling center or referral network; volunteer as a mentor in your area of expertise; organize self-help groups; use your psychological and/or medical expertise to help in church or para-church organizations; help start support groups; work to meet the needs of the church and community; befriend those who are hurting and help them follow through with therapy or mentoring; educate the church on biblical responses to contemporary emotional and social issues; and coordinate prayer, small groups and accountability partners for those seeking assistance.

Rating:		**1-5** (1 = not interested; 5 = very interested)

NOTES

_____

_____

_____

_____

_____

_____

_____

_____

_____

_____

_____

_____

_____

_____

_____

_____

_____

_____

_____

11. MUSIC MINISTRY

You believe that music is a gift and blessing used to praise God and create an atmosphere to receive the Holy Spirit. Through voice and the playing of instruments, you seek to inspire worship and thanksgiving and stir individuals to express their intimate emotions to God. While music has the potential to unify, you understand the conflict that can be generated from opposing opinions about the kinds and styles of music that should be used. Therefore, you're committed to being sensitive and respectful as you meet the needs of the congregation and accommodate diverse music preferences. You explore music's wide range of uses to the best of your ability and seek to glorify God in all that you do.

Areas of Ministry:
Lead or participate in the choir, band, or orchestra; teach singing, instruments, and music; help in marketing music programs and events; assist as a stagehand or in lights, or sound during music events; write music and/or lyrics; create or find arrangements for church performances and events; and perform with a musical group or as a soloist.

Rating:		**1-5** (1 = not interested; 5 = very interested)

NOTES

96

12. DRAMA/SPEECH MINISTRY

Christian drama deals with significant and vital themes of life, presenting characters in action in situations where faith and belief are tested. You believe that drama can make Bible stories and biblical principles come alive and seek to use it as an educational technique to inspire the church. You believe that writing and/or performing is a sacred trust and dedicate your craft to God and pray for his guidance. You're willing to lead, coordinate, and participate in script writing, rehearsals, costuming, stage layout, and other preparations to achieve a potentially significant impact on the lives of the participants and the audience. You make your skills available to groups in the church and are willing to coach and mentor others.

Areas of Ministry:

Lead, coordinate, or perform in skits and dramas to illustrate sermons or special services; work with the choir in performing a musical drama; write dramas, skits, and speeches to be used in the church; tutor young people in acting; entertain and inspire children, elderly, and special groups on a variety of topics; assist in designing and building sets; work as a stagehand; assist in lighting and sound; and sell tickets and help with event marketing.

Rating:		1-5 (1 = not interested; 5 = very interested)

NOTES

13. VISUAL ARTS MINISTRY

You believe that God is the original artist and has given us gifts of craftsmanship and creativity to be used to connect with God in a way that goes beyond words. You are passionate about using your creativity to help people open themselves to other dimensions of their lives by inspiring self-examination, contemplation, and awe. You use visual arts to raise awareness about social concerns that need the attention of the church. You see art as a form of worship and are dedicated to helping people relate to God with their whole selves, not just with their minds. You enjoy modeling the creative process in ways that help others use their own creativity to solve problems, plan projects, and strengthen relationships.

Areas of Ministry:
Express yourself through painting, crafts, photography, poetry, graphics, or other form of art; help beautify the church; advocate for and coordinate space in the church to exhibit artistic works; invite artists to speak on art and faith or art in the Bible; find ways to integrate art into church life; use graphics to help communicate church initiatives and events; design web site or presentation graphics; create murals; teach/tutor visual arts; create artwork to raise money; and use your art as a way to befriend someone.

Rating:		1-5 (1 = not interested; 5 = very interested)

NOTES

14. ADULT MINISTRY

The adult population of the church is the greatest and most diverse of any age because it can encompass seven or more decades. You have a passion for adult faith formation and discipleship that includes all adults and encourages them to grow and mature in faith. You have a burden to keep adults integrated and vibrant within the church so they may be vital disciples for a lifetime. You are a team player, enjoy working with other adults and understand adult development and generational differences. You recognize and celebrate the gifts, talents, and contributions of adults in your church and find ways to help them participate and remain active in the work of the Church during each season of life.

Areas of Ministry:
Sunday school teacher; host home group meetings; one-on-one discipleship; lead support groups for one of many topics relevant to the needs in church and community; mentor adults; teach marriage seminars; assist in parenting skill training; help those that are suffering; be a lay-pastor over a small group of adults; help with career setbacks; coordinate your services with others in the church; set up a career planning and job center in the church; be an adult counselor; host Bible fellowship group meetings; participate in home visitation; plan social activities for various adult groups; and advocate for, organize, or maintain an adult resource center.

Rating:		**1-5** (1 = not interested; 5 = very interested)

NOTES

15. COMPUTER TECHNOLOGY MINISTRY

You believe that wise use of technology will help build the Kingdom of God. You know there are very few church and ministry departments that are not partially or completely dependent on computers, and you have a passion for working with technology. You enjoy helping the church use computers to solve problems, save money, and better serve church members on the local level. You like to work with church and para-church leadership and ministry teams and use your skills to help implement an initiative for the glory of God.

Areas of Ministry:

Set up computer networks; design, develop and maintain websites; install software; teach software, PC, and mobile device skills to church and ministry staff; provide on-call help desk services; maintain and troubleshoot computer systems; participate in strategic planning by offering technical advice; create computerization implementation recommendations to maintain ongoing technology efficiencies and security; and set up a computer learning center.

Rating:		1-5 (1 = not interested; 5 = very interested)

NOTES

16. FOOD SERVICES MINISTRY

You believe that food provides the perfect opportunity for fellowship and ministry among church members, visitors, and guests. You have a passion for serving, encouraging, comforting, and supporting one another by preparing and serving food. You understand the importance of an efficient kitchen, an inviting fellowship hall, and serving comforting food in the right amounts for each event. You have a servant's heart and treasure the privilege of feeding God's people. You enjoy serving in a way that helps people see, sense, and experience that you care about them and that God loves them. You make sure that weddings, celebrations, funerals, conferences, daycare, and other events and ministries get the food services they need.

Areas of Ministry:

Participate on the food services committee; volunteer to plan, shop, cook, serve, or help clean up; help schedule and coordinate menus, cooks, and supplies for church events that need food services; help update and install new food service equipment; organize the kitchen pantry, refrigerator/freezer, and cooking supplies; post food services needs to the church events calendar to recruit volunteers and obtain donations; and mentor others with your food services expertise in kitchen organization, event planning, crowd cooking, and banquet serving skills.

Rating:		1-5 (1 = not interested; 5 = very interested)

NOTES

17. MEDIA MINISTRY

You have a passion to help create a spiritual and inspiring atmosphere for church services and ministry using audio, visual, and electronic technology. You enjoy using your technical gifts to help services and events lead people into a new or growing relationship with Christ. You like to help reinforce the message being delivered during praise and worship services, concerts, and other special programs by producing a high-quality experience for both the presenters and the audience. You enjoy using your skills to produce the best communications possible and reproduce services, sermons, and teaching for distribution and use on the internet and social media platforms. You like being part of expanding the effectiveness of church messages.

Areas of Ministry:

Research electronic, software and equipment; install, update, and maintain systems; operate audio/visual system for church services and events; operate the camera during rehearsals and events; edit and reproduce audio/visual files; create storyboards for pre-event/implementation planning sessions; design an electronic suite for the auditorium; and lead or participate on the media team.

Rating:		**1-5** (1 = not interested; 5 = very interested)

NOTES

18. MISSIONS MINISTRY

You believe that God has called the Church to go into the entire world to preach the gospel and as a church, we should be involved in missions. You advocate for and keep the cause of missions in the forefront by providing missionary updates to leadership, ministry groups, and the congregation. You make sure updates appear on the church website and are prevalent through social media. You keep a list of missionaries and pray for them each day during personal prayer time and at group prayer services. You enjoy helping missionaries on furlough by arranging speaking opportunities, coordinating housing and transportation needs, taking up collections for needs, and planning social events for fellowship and prayer.

Areas of Ministry:

Lead or participate on the missions committee; pray faithfully for missionaries; advocate for, organize, and lead a men's or women's group with a focus on supporting missionaries; solicit special offerings and gifts for missionary needs; collect and distribute supplies for missionaries in the field; help plan details of a missionary furlough; plan, coordinate, or participate in annual missions conferences; plan, coordinate or participate in short-term mission trips for members of the church; and update the church on missionary plans, trips, and events.

Rating:		1-5 (1 = not interested; 5 = very interested)

NOTES

_____

_____

_____

_____

_____

_____

_____

_____

_____

_____

_____

_____

_____

_____

_____

_____

_____

_____

_____

19. PASTORAL DUTIES MINISTRY

You believe lay leaders function as a role model of Christian discipleship and faith lived out in the church and in daily life. You work with the pastor to fulfill the mission and vision of the congregation and assist with leadership and the vision of the church. You believe preaching and teaching is a sacred call and you prepare diligently by praying and studying before you preach or teach the Word of God. You enjoy using your skills and experience to oversee the congregation or specialized groups such as youth, seniors, ex-offenders, the homeless, sports teams, or mission groups. You take time to be with God so you can be the person he wants you to be. You resist pride and strive to be a servant leader by being a good listener and communicating well with people of all ages. You trust God for your ministry and go where he is working. You enjoy assisting with the pastoral duties of visitation, comforting the hurting, welcoming visitors, and helping new people assimilate into the church.

Areas of Ministry:
Preach sermons; teach classes and seminars; oversee ministry groups; facilitate group discussions; assist with church administration; oversee the spiritual welfare of those entrusted to you; meet with people to pray with them; visit members of the church; perform weddings, funerals, dedications, baptisms, and communion; oversee homeless programs; oversee small groups; help plan and conduct church services and events; contribute to the vision of the church; conduct prayer services; and support/assist the pastor with leadership duties.

Rating:		1-5 (1 = not interested; 5 = very interested)

NOTES

20. LEISURE & RECREATION MINISTRY

You believe leisure and recreational activities can be intentional natural touch points for ministry to take place. You enjoy creating gathering places for people through recreation of all types. You know these events bridge cultural and racial barriers and build fellowship so the gospel message can be shared in word and by example. You have a passion to create activities that offer ways for the congregation to live out their abilities, interests, talents, and spiritual giftedness. You use your skills and experience to plan, coordinate, lead, coach and minister to the spiritual needs of active participants and their families.

Areas of Ministry:

Plan, coordinate and participate in regular activities and special events; assist with cultural events on campus; sports and cultural activities; plan and coordinate camping programs; plan and conduct activities for the senior day care program, AWANA, Brigade, and Pioneer programs; implement classes for community exercise, crafts and music; provide walking trails; provide space and support to after-school programs and the community; and stay up on community recreation programs and include use of the church when appropriate, such as Boy and Girl Scouts.

Rating:		1-5 (1 = not interested; 5 = very interested)

NOTES

PART TWO SCORING INSTRUCTIONS: Go back through Part Two (pages 77-96) and transfer your rating for each type of ministry to the scoring chart below.

	MINISTRY PREFERENCE	RATING
1	Youth	
2	Children	
3	Evangelism	
4	Visitation	
5	Community	
6	Office Administration	
7	Leadership	
8	Maintenance	
9	Christian Education	
10	Counseling/Mentoring	
11	Music	
12	Drama/Speech	
13	Visual Arts	
14	Adult	
15	Computer Technology	
16	Food Services	
17	Media	
18	Missions	
19	Pastoral Duties	
20	Leisure & Recreation	

■ MINISTRY PREFERENCE INVENTORY SUMMARY ■

INSTRUCTIONS: Based on the information you recorded in the Part One summary (Page 76) and the Part Two scoring chart (Page 97), determine your top three ministry preferences. Transfer this summary information to your **Personal Ministry Profile in** the workbook or e-form.

TOP THREE MINISTRY PREFERENCES

1 ....

2 ....

3 ....

PERSONAL MINISTRY PROFILE

Your Personal Ministry Profile

SKILLS   EDUCATION   EXPERIENCE   SPIRITUAL GIFTS   MINISTRY DRIVES   MINISTRY PREFERENCES

INSTRUCTIONS: List your preferred contact information and references in the sections provided below. As you complete each inventory in the workbook, transfer summary section information to this Personal Ministry Profile or the e-form version available for download at www.empowerministry.org/PMP.

PERSONAL INFORMATION
Preferred Contact Information

Last Name	First Name	MI	Email	
Street Address	City	ST	Zip	Phone
Church you attend (if applying outside your church)		Church Phone	Pastor's Name	

REFERENCES
Spiritual & Character References

Name	Relationship	Phone
Name	Relationship	Phone
Name	Relationship	Phone
Name	Relationship	Phone

SKILLS
Skill Inventory Summary (Page 13)

1
2
3
4
5

EDUCATION
Education Inventory Summary (Page 16)

_____
_____
_____
_____

EXPERIENCE
Experience Inventory Summary (Page 19)

_____
_____
_____

SPIRITUAL GIFTS
Spiritual Gift Inventory Summary (Page 49)

Part One: Ministry Task

_____
_____

Part Two: Service Opportunity Descriptions

_____
_____
_____

Part Three: Equipping Roles

_____
_____

MINISTRY DRIVES
Ministry Drive Inventory Summary (Page 70)

1 _____
2 _____
3 _____
4 _____

MINISTRY PREFERENCES
Ministry Preference Inventory Summary (Page 97)

1 _____
2 _____
3 _____

EMPOWER MINISTRY
12540 S. 68th Court, Palos Heights IL 60463
ron@empowerministry.org   708.601.01

WIRED for MINISTRY

CONCLUSION

The Final Step

This has been a detailed, reflective process, but now you have a better understanding of how God uniquely created you for ministry. Now you're ready to meet with ministry leaders at your church or the director of volunteer services at your favorite charity to identify specific volunteer opportunities. You're looking for ways that will take full advantage of your gifts and abilities and allow you to serve the Lord in a way that energizes you and brings you deep joy. And organizations are looking for qualified volunteers.

What's next? Now you're ready to decide which ministries you would like to volunteer for and how you would like to share the information you've collected. It's a good idea for you to print your completed Personal Ministry Profile, assemble your "resume," and make an appointment with ministry leaders at your church or the director of volunteer services at your favorite charity.

PREPARE FOR THE INTERVIEW

The organization may be very casual or may have specific procedures for meeting with you. They may ask you to submit information prior to your appointment so they can review it before they meet with you. Bring enough copies for everyone in the meeting and follow the same protocol you would in applying for employment. Be prompt, respectful of their time, dress appropriately, and act professionally.

Organizations interview volunteers for many reasons. They want to make sure the volunteer is going to be a good fit with the organization and use the interview to gather information from the volunteer. In addition to getting information, they want to give the volunteer sufficient information to make a decision about volunteering for the organization. The decision to volunteer should be a two-way street. After this exchange of information, they'll have a better idea of whether there is a match between what is needed/offered by the organization and the potential volunteer.

Conducting formal interviews shows an organization takes volunteer involvement seriously and is an important part of recruiting and retaining quality volunteers. By the end of the interview, they will be confident that they know what you expect from working with their organization and exactly why you want to get involved. This will let them know if it's a good fit and will heavily influence their decision about engaging you as a volunteer.

Expect the interviewer to ask questions that will help them determine what tasks are appropriate for you based on your interests, skills, knowledge, and experience. They also need to identify any limitations that might affect the tasks you can undertake, such as your availability.

As you prepare for the interview, remember that you are God's masterpiece! Our great and loving God thought about you individually and then intentionally created you for specific good works. Be confident in what you have learned about yourself and be ready to share that information in the interview.

STANDARD VOLUNTEER INTERVIEW QUESTIONS

- What interested you about this volunteer position?
- Is there an aspect of our mission that motivates you to want to volunteer?
- Tell me the story of how you chose your education program, career path or life work.
- Have you volunteered in the past?
    - Yes: What did you enjoy most about previous volunteer work?
    - No: What have you enjoyed most about previous paid work or other activities?
- Are you involved in other organized activities?
- What special skills would you like us to utilize as a volunteer?
- Are there tasks that you don't want to do as a volunteer?
- Briefly talk about your experience as it relates to this position.
- What are three of your strengths?
- Do you prefer working independently or with a group?
- What is the ideal volunteer job for you, and why?
- Describe your ideal supervisor.
- What are your expectations of our organization? Of our employees?
- What are your personal goals for this experience?
- Do you have any concerns about what we expect from you?
- Are you willing to make a time commitment of _____ ?
- Are you interested in training pertinent to this position?
- Are you willing to provide training in your area of expertise to other volunteers or staff members?
- Do you have any questions that you would like to ask us?

You Matter

If I could only use two words to end this book, I would sum it up this way…you matter! You matter to God and you matter to this world. We are obsessed with celebrity status in this country. We put too much emphasis on a few people. This obsession tells us that if we aren't the best, the brightest, the richest, the best looking or famous, then we don't count; we don't really matter. Yet for all the attention, all the glory and all the focus of the world, today's movie stars, models, singers, and athletes are simply tomorrow's forgotten headlines.

The truth is, we are afraid of *ordinariness*. We are afraid of being "just another brick in the wall" (Pink Floyd, *The Wall*, 1979). The fact is, you'll never be a brick. You're a billion times more complicated, intricate and unique than that. Even with your sameness to others, your common appearance and existence, you're still uniquely significant! You have a role in life that is important to this world. You have value. You matter and what you do matters!

In the first chapter, we stated that each of us has a mission in this world. We wrote that personal ministry is to live with the awareness of the risen Christ; using our personhood, gifts, and skills to serve him in everything we do. In this workbook, we've helped you identify your ministry drives, spiritual gifts and ministry preferences. We also helped you discover how you were wired for a lifetime of ministry through your personality, skills, education, and experiences. Our conclusion is that God has fully equipped you for his service.

We've prepared you…now it is up to you. What are you going to do with all that you've discovered? What are you going to do with everything that God has spoken to your heart about during this process? Our challenge to you is to take all that you've learned and let God lead you. Start today to trust him, to ask him to empower you for the ministries that he has for you. Ask him for guidance, wisdom, and the strength to get started. I encourage you to take advantage of Page 105, Reflection and Action Planning, to record what you've learned during this process and how you'll put this knowledge into action.

May God bless you as you enjoy a life of service for God.

Looking for a devotional book that speaks to your deepest needs?

MOMENT IN THE WORD
Daily Moments That Feed Your Soul

With a prolific career in both ministry and social causes, Ron Ovitt has provided a year-long collection of devotionals that will guide to praise, reflection, and worship. Different than most devotional books, *Moment in the Word* **speaks to everyday emotions and brings God's Word to encourage, comfort, and console.**

Join the thousands of others who make *Moment in the Word* a part of their daily journey.

Ron Ovitt, *Moment in the Word*

GILGAL
PUBLISHING

AVAILABLE ON AMAZON

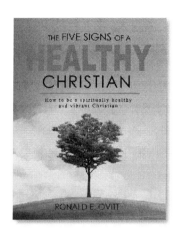

Health is on everyone's mind. Are you a healthy Christian?

THE FIVE SIGNS OF A HEALTHY CHRISTIAN
How to Be a Spiritually Healthy and Vibrant Christian

Our personal health, the health of our nation, the health of our economy—all with good reason. When things are unhealthy, bad things start to happen. But what about the health of our Christian experience? *The Five Signs of a Healthy Christian* will lead you to investigate your own spiritual health and encourage you to make adjustments where necessary.

There are five signs that are general indicators that we are spiritually alive. **If you keep focused on these factors, praying over them and taking baby steps toward improving where needed, you will find yourself living a healthy Christian life!**

This book will help motivate and encourage you in maintaining a deep and meaningful spiritual life.

Ron Ovitt, *The Five Signs of a Healthy Christian*

GILGAL
PUBLISHING

Made in the USA
Middletown, DE
29 September 2018